Wake up to who you really are!
You are the one you have been waiting for...

Dig Deep
&
Fly High

Reclaim Your Zest and Vitality
by Loving Yourself from Inside Out

BY PENELOPE AELFIN

Penelope Aelfin
PO Box 972
Mona Vale
New South Wales
Australia 1660

Limits of Liability and Disclaimer of Warranty

Warning—Disclaimer

ISBN: 978-0-9923188-8-8

Dig Deep
&
Fly High!

Reclaim Your Zest and Vitality
by Loving Yourself from Inside Out

By Penelope Aelfin

"At any moment, you have a choice that either leads you closer to your spirit or further away from it."

~ Thich Nhat Hanh

Dedication

This book is dedicated to my father.

After he passed away, his invisible presence whilst developing myself
along my journey has been a powerful and potent ally.
It was only when he died I came to the understanding of
how deep a bond we had.

I miss you, Pop; this is for you!

Acknowledgments

This book, *Dig Deep & Fly High!,* is the pinnacle of yet another jumping-off point that I have come to in my life.

It brings together all my experiences, lessons learned, and wisdom gained over my life so far, the journey and integration of which would not have been possible without some very special people supporting me along the way.

I would like to thank my mother and father for choosing to have another child in their lives and giving me an appreciation of the beauty of my surroundings; my sister and brother for always being there; and their families, though they are far away. Sister Wilkins, my nanny, and Auntie Von, who provided me their safe presence when needed and who were so full of kindness, cuddles, love, and laughter.

There have been some very important milestones reached and bridges that I have crossed in my life. I would like to thank the following people in particular, as they were very much my wakeup call and people who inspired me to do well and supported me along the way.

Evan Lallemand, who was instrumental in getting my health back; Per Neuman and Leonard Lauder, who gave me the strength to believe in my capacity and skills in my corporate life; Sally Challenor, who encouraged me to express my creativity in establishing my own interior design business; Terry Lipman, who accepted me for who I was, warts and all, and for being my guardian angel over time; Shoshana Faire and John Denver, who introduced me to sustainability and another way of living in this world.

My teachers along the way, Andrew Verity and Geraldine Gallagher, for their skills and knowledge about kinesiology and the well-being they imparted; Glynn Brady, for knowledge of the mysteries of life; Walter and Gita Bellin, who opened me up to glimpses of my spirit; Dr. Joanna Martin, who believed in what I could not see in myself; Lynx Raven, who got me; Jade Richardson, who was so instrumental in re-opening my creativity, Baeth Davis, who gave me the courage to fly; and Donna Kozik, who made the next step possible.

My spiritual teachers, who held my hand along my personal questing; Autori, for holding the space to experience my light; Kaliana Raphael Rose, for showing me her softness and open heart; Nicole Cody, for her continual caring and love; Elayne Doughty, for her total belief in who I am at my core; Jennifer Starlight and Min, for waking me up that I needed to fly off the cliff.

To the two men I married, Otto Kiow and Tony Ward taught me hard but essential and valuable lessons; and to Roger Harman, the man who gave me the gift of opening my heart. Thank you for your gifts.

And my deepest thanks go to those friends who are always there, whatever the situation. I call them my tribe. Margie Evans, Pammie Williams, Tracey Hemmy, Aquila Faenza, Greg Dutton, Michael Katz, Lily de Chalain, Celia Esplin, Pauline Abel, Merry Pearson, Donna Etchells, Patricia Janssen, and my newfound friends in Bali, Lynne Chelin, Nancy Foss, Trudy Mackenzie, Fiona Bailey, Anna Guppy, and Linda Madani. In particular, I would like to thank my two Fairy Godmothers, Marion Vaughan, for holding my space in times of crisis, and Tema Sines, who has been so instrumental in holding my hand as I put the final pieces of me back together.

There are many others I know and I don't often see, and others I have met along the way, where paths have crossed briefly and profoundly. You know who you are.

Thank you deeply and profoundly from the bottom of my heart for your gifts, your time, your wisdom and friendship. Words cannot express the appreciation I feel.

I want to give thanks to all of humanity. We can live in a better world and I look forward to us co-creating this together.

"What if… What if our religion was each other, if our practice was our life, if prayer our words? What if the temple was the Earth, if forests were our church, if holy waters - the rivers lakes and oceans? What if meditation was our relationships, if the teacher was life, if wisdom was self-knowledge, if love was the centre of our being?"

~ Ganga White

How Can I Help You?

"When I stand in the truth of who I am, I no longer fear to begin again."

~ Tom Lescher

My experience serves me well to do this work. I hold your hand, nurture you along the path, listen to your story, and assist you to navigate through the maze that maybe in front of you and assist you to integrate the pieces. I serve humanity through understanding love.

I am a teacher, mentor, and guide of universal principles.

To get you started on your journey right away, get your free copy of my ***Daily Mindset Reboot*** action plan now, "***Stop Being Stuck in The Rut Spinning Your Wheels***". It will keep you out of overwhelm.

It's easy.

Just go to my website at **www.HealYourSeparation.com** and click on the link!

My experience, gained on my own life journey through being physically sick and encumbered, and moving to a new country to experience life differently, made me look into the depths of myself to heal my pain and find my diamond. Working with many clients over the years and seeing them grow into their potential and shine, too, I have something to offer you that will support your soul to come alive and let your spirit shine through.

I support people in finding their real self, giving order to chaos and spotlighting the inner beauty to shine assisting transition through turbulent times.

I offer a variety of packages to support and assist people on their journey. I invite you to check in at my website:

www.HealYourSeparation.com

Some of the benefits you will receive by reading **Dig Deep & Fly High!** *are:*

- Gain clarity about your sacred wounds.

- Receive assistance to look inward to your truth.

- Support you to understand how to take your next steps.

- Help with building a new life for yourself.

- Learn tips and tools of the spiritual journey.

- Follow the path of an experienced traveler.
  Become your own spiritual mama!

I look forward to our journey together.

Go to **www.HealYourSeparation.com**
And get your free copy of my Daily Mindset Reboot
"Stop Being Stuck in The Rut Spinning Your Wheels"

About the Author

For the past 25 years, Penelope Aelfin's experience has been gained in the human potential field and alternative health arena. She has worked with individuals and groups exploring the field of awareness and personal development. Previous to that, she worked in the corporate arena in the fashion and cosmetics industries, in both the retail and wholesale sectors. For 15 years she ran her own commercial interior design business.

In her early 20s Penelope's personal poor health sparked a journey into inner self-discovery, and today she enjoys premium health, a sense of freedom, inner peace, and love.

Her greatest passion is to support you on your own inner personal journey, and as a collective we can enjoy freedom and peace of mind, and live in a loving, harmonious world.

Testimonials

"Penelope's intuition and compassion are palpable—she lives what she works, and it is obvious in the wonderful results I've watched her achieve over the years. She holds the space for you to explore, transform and discover parts of yourself in a new way, find your mojo and come alive to your creative expression."
~ **Dena Sharrock, anthropologist**

"I have worked with Penelope for a very short period of time and I have been absolutely thrilled to have such an intuitive, creative person on my side. Penelope is like a breath of fresh air just when you need it. Her insightful words calm the spirit providing you with the courage to take 'the right next steps.' Penelope is a visionary for helping others to manifest their world. Our relationship will continue to grow based on intuition, ease, joy and glory. What else is possible?"
~ **Nancy Foss, marketing vision consultant**

"Penelope is a compassionate and effective practitioner. I really appreciate her ability to bring humour and lightness of spirit to her work."
~ **Victoria Keys, Hakomi practitioner**

"Penelope, a few words to tell you that you have enriched my life; and I am sure many others. You have helped me get thru some difficult days, and for that I am truly grateful.
You have a gift, so please keep sharing it."
~ **Lynne Chelin, business consultant**

"I have used her skills as a kinesiologist for both myself and my children, who find her very approachable. She has enormous energy and compassion for people. She creates a safe, caring and supportive space so you can go forward."

~ **Margie Evans, spiritual mentor**

"I am so very grateful I allowed myself to trust Penelope with my deepest fears and blocks I hold within myself. She with her years of practice and experience in kinesiology and a true understanding of how deep life's accumulated pain is held at a cellular level, through one session and many supportive conversations afterwards she showed me a precious door to walk through towards a much required journey of self-acknowledgment and healing."

~ **Fiona Bailey, yoga instructor**

"Penelope gave me practical skills but she also mined my past for the things that were holding me back. Since seeing Penelope I have written 10 books and achieved virtually all my career and personal goals."

~ **Nikki Goldstein, author**

"Penelope has developed a way of communicating with the body's energetic system that is sensitive, accurate, therapeutic, and enlightening. Her method of kinesiology clearly demonstrates what so many holistic and energetic medicine practitioners aspire to: the next paradigm of healing, the energetic paradigm. I have been fortunate to be both a recipient of Penelope's healing and a student of her method. Both have been an integral part of my development as a practitioner of holistic medicine and a being in this world."

~ **Tjok Gde Kerthyasa, BHSc(Hom.), ADHom., homeopath**

Contents

Hi,

I am glad that you are here!

Congratulations for taking the leap to explore your life on another level. It takes tremendous courage to want to change your life for the better, to face the truth of who you are. Allowing yourself to release what doesn't work or is no longer useful to you in your life, and to adopt new foundational guidelines and strategies, is a gigantic step. I am thrilled to accompany you on this journey, the benefits and rewards of which are many.

In the third-dimensional world, life is never static. There is always change; that is a given. It can be confronting! Life comes with its ups and downs; the challenges of which are different and varied, and are always there to assist your growth and expansion. So whatever is your particular angst, I look forward to sharing different ways to assist you forward.

Through this book, I give you guidance in how to see your life differently, and share various tools you can use and put into practice on a daily basis. I give you:

- Questions to prompt inquiry into what influences you in your life right now.

- Different tools you can use to gain more clarity and be more powerful.

- Actions steps that allow you to expand your awareness, let go of thoughts, behaviors, emotions, and struggles that no longer are appropriate, enabling you to go with your natural flow of life.

- Tools to learn how to be your own spiritual mama.

I share with you universal principles to use as foundational tools for your life, guidance in how to design your new awareness pathway that reflects your soul, inner essence and spark, and simple strategies that you can adopt on a daily basis to support you on your way.

There are some turbulent times coming in the world for you and me;

1

in fact, they are here already. In the times ahead you need to find that place inside of you of trust and love in who you are, so you can feel centered, point your compass in the right direction, and be your own guide and authority. I am optimistic; I do see a bright future past the chaos, and it probably won't happen overnight. I envisage a diverse world where we are all seen and celebrated for our uniqueness and differences, and I look forward to it.

Right now is the time to work on you, awaken and give birth to your true self, polish yourself up, and be your beauty from inside out. Be the lighthouse beacon and shine brightly, come out to play, sparkle with zest, and let your life source energy flow, because you know what? Ultimately there is only one edition of you!

Please enjoy this information and your journey. I wish you magic along the way, and a new way of being that makes you shine.

"Your journey is a blessing and
a blessing is a bridge between heaven and earth."

~ Penelope Aelfin

Love, Light, and Blessings,

Penelope Aelfin

Penelope's Story

"I am strong, because I have been weak

I am fearless, because I have been afraid

I am wise, because I've been foolish."

~ Anonymous

My Early Beginnings

My life began in the late 1940s in England in a small village in the country. There were five of us in my family. I am the youngest of three, and I have an older sister and brother. There were many years apart between us, and I often felt like an only child, as my siblings were off doing their thing, which was more appropriate to their age group.

I lived in a small community with nature surrounding me. In summer I loved nothing more than to be in the large garden full of beautifully scented flowers, rose bushes, and two large beech trees watching butterflies flutter and bees buzz and pollinate. I was mesmerized.

There was a very abundant vegetable garden, an orchard full of chickens, different fruit trees of varying heights (lending themselves to my climbing activities and sitting in the tree tops watching the world go by), succulent bushes of different-colored berries to eat, and greenhouses growing more exotic items.

I loved this garden in the summer and as a small girl continually played in this haven. I often ventured out to the woods beyond, where my favorite pastime in spring was to sit among the bluebells, spread around me like a carpet.

During the summer months my family spent many an idle day by the sea, watching the tides come in and out, and the wave patterns as they crashed to the shoreline. We built numerous sandcastles until the waves washed them away again. I learned how to search for cockles and winkles, set eel lines, catch crabs, and other mysterious activities. My heart was happy and singing.

While this was beautiful and I loved that part of my life, my love of nature became my mainstay and escape. I was born into a conservative family, with rules and regulations of how to behave, with the shoulds and shouldn'ts of the world, the rights and wrongs.

Only later did I recognize I did not feel free to express myself as me; my expression and delight of the world of fairies were not always appreciated! I was thought of as too lively and noisy, and not the well-behaved child. I was continually pulled into line.

I know my parents did love me, but it wasn't always expressed to me in the way I understood. Rather than hugs and affection and understanding, I was given rules, disciplines, and punishments, presumably to keep me safe and controlled. I spent many a day in my room!

At the time, I felt ashamed about who I was and not safe in the world. I did not trust myself, and others, or my surroundings, and I felt abandoned. I soon learned as a child the game was to be seen and not heard! After a while I began to see myself as unlovable and not important.

Teenage Years and My Education

I was sent away to a girls' boarding school at the age of 11, where I spent five years. I found this to be an even harsher environment than home and found it difficult to fit in and belong. My feelings of shame and not belonging continued, and I started to doubt myself and my abilities. As a result, I hid my light from the world.

I was brought up in an era when it was expected that girls would marry and have children (not a career, as being a housewife and mother was the path). When it came to choosing a career path, my parents offered me two options: nursing or secretarial! I took the secretarial route, as it gave me more freedom in the university town where I learned those skills.

My real dream was to go to art school and become a dress designer or graphic artist. My parents feared that I would become a beatnik and would not be able to get employment. The rebel in me became the beatnik while I was doing my secretarial training. (Hey, it was the '60s; we all needed to break out of the mold!)

I was following the family pattern of conforming to what was expected rather than my dreams. Both of my parents were extremely creative people who gave up on their dreams early in life and did what was expected of them by their family and community.

Late Teens and Early 20s

During my late teens, the stress of not being allowed to express my true nature in my short life came to light. My health suffered with a chronic case of arthritis, which I managed with prescription drugs to take away the pain, only for it resurface again a few months later. This continued off and on for 10 years until I found another way.

Earning my own money and being in the workforce gave me some type of freedom. I was enticed by travel. I would travel for months at a time, and occasionally come home to roost, gathering my energies only to go off again on another adventure—always seeking, and using this as an escape from reality and my pain.

In my mid-20s I rebelled and struck out. I married someone who was not thought of as an appropriate match, and it was definitely not given the stamp of approval. My father refused to come to the wedding, and my husband and I were banned from going home for a year. This compounded my feeling of not being important and lovable, as I was so isolated from my family.

The Start of a New Journey

To escape, we migrated to Australia—12,000 miles away, to the other side of the earth. In all reality I was running away from home! Australia for me was like an oasis, where I began to blossom and over the years find my own way in life. I learned that I was able to be more of who I was, and over time my prickliness, sharp edges, and self-imposed limitations started to fall away.

One of my biggest stepping stones was to handle my health in a different way. Up to that point I only knew about doctors and medication; I had no knowledge of other healing methods.

I was about to join an international company—a dream opportunity—when I had another attack of crippling arthritis. Due to this incident I started to look into different avenues of healing available. I was supported by a wonderful acupuncturist, who led me to discover a broader view of health from a mental, emotional, physical, and spiritual perspective—a wonderful gift, in hindsight, as this painful experience led me to a wonderful gift of healing and opportunity to set me on a whole new way of living.

I was unable to move either my fingers or my toes (they were rigid), walk on my feet, or hold a knife or fork without screaming with pain. At my first acupuncture treatment I was amazed by how quickly the pain dissipated. It took only15 minutes for my fingers and toes to start moving and for the pain to start to disappear. I was ecstatic, and tears of appreciation ran down my face.

At that point my life changed forever: I made the decision I never ever wanted to experience that kind of pain again, and I would do whatever it took in my life to heal myself and unravel the cause.

I learned that health comprises not only the physical body; it also includes your emotional, mental, and spiritual state of being. I changed the food I ate, exercised more, and started to explore my emotional and mental state of being, which led me to learn about other various health modalities.

I worked in my corporate job for 10 years and loved it. To succeed I turned myself inside out, and there came a time when I did not like whom I was becoming in myself and my heart. I was not happy. The stress of this was enormous, my body started to give me signs that all was not right by sending those arthritic twinges and pain again, and my immune system was being affected.

Going out on My Own

So to another important landmark in my life, I took the plunge, left the corporate arena, and started to work for myself. At the same time I delved into a lifetime of learning about my spiritual expression and who I was deep down. This led me into the mystical world of shamanism, crystals, and other energy healing methods while I was also doing other personal development programs. I reckon I have a PhD in personal development seminars since I have attended so many!

I then discovered kinesiology, which is the study of the body in motion, and includes all areas of physical, emotional, mental, and spiritual aspects. Muscle testing or muscle monitoring is used to communicate on a deep level with the body's truth.

I was so enamored of the results that happened for me and the ways in which it was supporting my own personal health that I ended up becoming a professional kinesiologist and facilitator. Added to these skills, I learned other counseling and spiritual healing techniques, knowledge about herbs, homeopathy, crystals, and naturopathy. I also became certified in trainings of conflict resolution and neuro-linguistic programming (NLP).

The other side of my life was the desire to be creative in an artistic sense. I ran my own my commercial interior design practice, relishing in my sense of color, beauty, and space, and applying the art of feng shui to all projects. I was able to support my love of nature and develop my skills in eco-sustainable design practices.

So I worked the two areas, which were very complementary of my talents, side by side. I thought I was made!

I had married for a second time, a fairytale wedding, light and magical, that I believed was forever! This was a very different experience from the first wedding, which had a brooding, dark, gothic theme.

Life was wonderful for the first seven or eight years, and then my spirit had other plans, taking me in another direction with more lessons, learning, and opportunities to be experienced.

Dark Night of the Soul

I went through a "dark night of the soul" period. As it descended upon me I went from disaster to disaster over a period of 10 years. I lost both my parents in a matter of eight months, and I felt my loss heavily. I went through menopause, which is not something that happens overnight; it is a two-, three-, or even five-year period of time for some people, and it is not an easy time for women. It can be quite emotional, and the woman you know can turn into another creature; some of us can turn into monsters! My husband had a heart attack. I lost my inheritance that I had invested to ensure there would be safety in the future. I went bankrupt. Our business failed. I had problems with my health, which deteriorated. My husband left me for another woman and we divorced. I used to say that I was deep down in Alice in Wonderland's rabbit hole with no way out!

As you can see, as my life journey progressed. I thought I was being given more evidence that I was not good enough and not lovable, through repeated patterns of despair in relationships and what I had created in my life.

It all sounds like such a sad tale, and others have their own equally tragic stories. My understanding now is that it was only a story. The signposts were staring at me loud and clear: I was going the wrong way, but I was not picking up on the signs. In each of the disasters, there was a wonderful opportunity, if only I could see it.

The fears that were keeping me stuck needed to be faced, and that word *shame* came back to hit me with such a force that it was not the time to go into denial or run away. I was feeling lost and frightened. It was time for me to face the music and see what was there. It was time to delve deep, deeper than ever before, to that place deep inside—the very core of my being.

Again my health was suffering; I had no energy and no motivation, and my passion had eluded me. I was totally burned out and was finding it increasingly difficult to work with clients. It felt like I was losing all my life-force and was slowly energetically disappearing from my life. At that time I think I would gladly have welcomed death. Life on this planet was too painful.

My Healing

At that time I was lucky enough to find my way into the presence of a spiritual teacher who taught me about letting the light into my life, allowing me to reconnect with the spiritual aspect of myself, gently healing, and bringing me back to my essence. It was so simple and very profound.

Very soon after this time I made a decision, another important milestone. With my energy back in full swing, I packed up my apartment, put everything in storage, and went overseas for seven weeks. I jumped off the cliff and started to fly, not knowing in what direction it would lead me.

I spent some time in Egypt, a country that had called me for years. It was spectacular. Many memories flooded back to me of other times I had spent there. It was there, late at night in the temple of Luxor, that I made the commitment to serve the light, to honor and know myself, and to be true to me, my true essential nature.

In this break, away from the humdrum existence of my life, it became crystal clear that I was being given an overview of the previous 10-year period. I came to the realization that how I had been struggling (trying to make ends meet, being in a marriage for too long that served neither party, feeling very unhappy and unfulfilled, and being fearful of the future) was not aligned with my spirit or purpose—and not an accurate picture of my truth.

Once I was able to claw my way out of the rabbit hole, see my story for what it was, and release some of the emotional attachment to failure, the wonderful gifts of that time became apparent.

My Life Now

For the last few years I have been on a path of delightful true exploration, and I feel that I have now come to understand what it is to slow down and "be" me—be peaceful in the knowledge that I am enough in just my being of who I am; and allow myself to be open, vulnerable, and loving to myself and others; face my fears (yes, they still say "hi" from time to time); and feel a sense of joy and fullness in my heart daily. It feels as though I have come to a place and time in my life where I am more of an authentic being, and that expressing my truth and being my essential nature is the only way.

The lessons I have learned have been varied and important, such as honoring, caring, respecting, and empowering myself, and acknowledging and getting off my drama story. For me there is one *vital* element, which is the foundation of all of these: learning to *love myself unconditionally*—a daily practice, and my key to a peaceful and joyful existence.

I have had the honor of being able to support many people on this journey of self-discovery, helping them rise above their woes and see their light; put money in their bank account; and attract and create the relationships they want and turning their life around.

I am not going to say this journey is easy. Each day is like a new slate, and it is a test to stay present, be aware and an observer of my life, to keep surrendering to what is, and go with the flow. It is an amazing journey with rich rewards. I would not change it for a moment!

Introduction

"Stop battling with your humanness
for it is an exquisite expression of God."

~ Jennifer Starlight

Do you feel as though something is missing in your life and that things are not connecting for you? Is your work life boring and do you feel tired on waking? Do you feel that people and you never come together on the same level? People just seem to come and go? Generally are you feeling lost and unanchored in your life? Your money situation should be better? You just need a big boost? Are you missing out on family life? Are you feeling stressed? You just don't seem to be able to get your life back on track and get things together?

It doesn't have to be that way. What I do is assist you to dig deep into what is keeping you stuck, what is giving you pain, and where your challenges are, supporting you to accept and release the pain and anguish, and clearing the way to a brighter future and a life that shines—a life where you come into your full potential, be the love and the divine spark you are, taking your rightful place in the human race, and exploring and expressing your talents, your gifts, and your dreams.

You, too, can have this joy for yourself. There will be a spring in your step and a smile on your face! Read on.

Section One

Knowing Who You Are and What You Are Not!

Chapter 1

Waking Up to Who You Really Are A Divine Spiritual Being

You are who you have been waiting for

"There is nothing in a caterpillar that tells you it's going to be a butterfly."

~ Buckminster Fuller

Who are you? Why are you here on earth? What is your soul's purpose?

You are all energy. Energy is made up of particles of light. Light is pure consciousness or awareness. Pure consciousness is love. You are all love. The source of all love is the heart. Inherently, you are an individual divine spark of God. By being born you deserve a place on this earth to express your radiance, your magnificence. It is a gift. You are a gift.

Your essential nature is spirit. Like all other living things, your life force energy is fed by light. You are also human. So you could describe yourself as spirit having a human experience!

You are part of the collective energy of spirit, and an individual on a soul basis, both interconnected. The divine is your inner knowing, love is who you are and your expression, and your experience is of the infinite intelligence.

You came to this planet for a "higher purpose"—that is, to evolve and grow. You are here to fulfill your potential, to learn how to be the ultimate human, and to live from your essence with wisdom. You are here to love unconditionally, to let go of your attachments and your beliefs, to let go and surrender to all that is, and to see your magnificence and the truth of your essence!

As Deepak Chopra states in his book *Creating Affluence,* when describing the Universal Law of Pure Potentiality, "we are all infinite creativity, pure potentiality and pure consciousness. Pure consciousness is spiritual essence unbounded. We are at our core in perfect balance, infinite silence, invincible, simplicity and bliss. This is our true essential nature."

Unless you are in touch with your spiritual essence as you take this journey, your experience can be one of struggle and a deep sense of loss through your lack of connection. By becoming separate from your essential nature, your individual growth becomes hampered. It is up to each individual to move forward, ultimately benefiting the collective growth.

As a child, part of you comes into this world as pure innocence. You are connected to both the material world and the metaphysical or supernatural realm; this is your natural state. As you progress through your childhood and come to adult life, your connection to the metaphysical gradually erodes away.

You have learned through your experiences not to trust these elements of yourself that, as a child, came naturally manifested as a connection to nature and nature spirits, enormous imagination with invisible playmates, heightened communication to the mystical, and a deep knowledge and trust of the world around you.

Life expressed through a child connected to universal consciousness and energy flow, when untouched by trauma, is pure magic.

In her book *Living in the Light,* Shakti Gawain explains the transformation of consciousness within each individual and in the world. She states: "Spirit is the essence of life, the energy of the universe that creates all things. Each one of us is a part of that spirit—a divine entity. So the spirit is the higher Self, the eternal being that lives within us."

It is time for you to have a true relationship with yourself, from the inside out. It is time to wake up from the social hypnosis and illusion around you. It is time to wake up to the truth of what you really are—no more denial or avoidance. Give yourself the gift of the presence of who you are. Heed the language of the heart; it is the healer. Value yourself just for being who you are in the moment, not as a consequence of your external world. You are perfect the way you are, if only you could see and feel it!

The evolution of the planet is on the brink of a massive expansion. It is a very exciting time to be alive: sitting on the cliff, ready to fly, wings outstretched to take off. The time has passed for you to play hide-and-seek with your soul and your unique expression!

What is the gift you have to give the world? What is your spiritual purpose—the agenda of your soul? It is waiting for you, like a flower yet to bloom.

This time is an invitation to open to your fullness and your radiant presence. The emergence of your essence is like the blossoming of a beautiful flower or a magnificent butterfly emerging from the chrysalis, ready for full flight into your true expression. You are special in the eyes of God; you are a spark of God, powerful beyond all measure.

You are spirit in human form, here to expand your awareness, connect with the deepest part of you to play, create, and have fun. Be true to your essence, reclaim your divine nature, your radiant spark, and be it! Live fully in love—*be love*. It is the true glue that holds you and the world together. You are who you have been waiting for!

Remember: Live a life worth living,
by living from the inside out!

Chapter 2

The Long-Term Consequences of Stress the Basis of Dis-ease

The costs of not being who you are

"Surrender to what is. Let go of what was. Have faith in what will be."

~ Sonia Ricotti

Stress is the number-one cause of illness and death in the world and the creation of dis-ease in society. It costs billions of dollars to deal with the outcome of ill health and hospitalization, not to mention the cost to businesses in both productivity and lost days at work, and the added stress this creates for family members.

The base problem of stress is the internal picture that you hold about yourself and your world, which is supported by your fears, emotions, beliefs, attitudes, and decisions. These are stored at a deep subconscious level in childhood. When feeling threatened, these feelings send signals to your nervous system to go into a reaction of a fight or flight behavior, an attack or withdrawal reaction. Fight is about attack and defense behavior. Flight is about running away and withdrawing from the situation. This has a flow on effect for the adrenals to be on physical hyper alert. If you live from this space on a continuing basis, you leave space for dis-ease and illness to develop at the part of you that is your weakest link. As Alex Collier so rightly states, *"The love you withhold is the pain you carry."*

Your inner landscape is not the only way you experience stress. In today's environment there are other hidden stresses. Below I list the various areas of stress that can affect humans.

Your Inner World and Stress

The decisions you made to keep you safe and secure about life, and the beliefs that get laid down at an early age in childhood go straight to your subconscious and are stored as in a hard drive on a computer. As your physical, mental, emotional and spiritual bodies are all interconnected, it is all the more important to find out what is buried deep down.

On a consciousness basis your brain is made up of two parts: the conscious and subconscious brain. Interestingly, your conscious brain comprises of only 10 percent of the total mind, and the subconscious the remaining 90 percent. Liken it to an iceberg: Conscious awareness is the tip of the iceberg, while the subconscious is the ice hidden under the water.

The conscious mind includes all that you are aware about. It is responsible for your logic and the rational thinking processes, your way of retrieving, filtering, and storing those pieces of information.

The subconscious contains all that is hidden. Stored in this area are your past painful experiences, made up of beliefs, fears, decisions, anxieties, emotions, resistances, and conflicts. This part of you has a tremendous influence on your attitudes and behaviors, and how you live and operate in the world on a day-to-day basis. Let's call them your unconscious drivers.

You are often unknowingly directed in your pursuit of life by these unconscious drivers, and then a major problem can emerge when the conscious and subconscious are in conflict with each other.

The concepts explored in psycho-neuro-immunology report a clear connection among your emotional state and your nervous system, immune functions, and the health of your organs, glands, and body systems. What is important to remember is you make choices with the 10 percent of your conscious mind, whereas your subconscious mind, the other 90 percent, only reacts to what is happening and has no choice.

When the body goes into stress over fears, emotional beliefs, and mental decisions with the unhealthy beliefs, your body goes into stress and responds by releasing a chemical reaction that releases neurotransmitters, affecting your immune system and the internal state of your body, which is there to keep you balanced and healthy.

If you are having fun and doing things you enjoy in life, it uplifts your energy and releases endorphins—the good chemicals! If you are having a down time, feeling depressed, are angry or sad, or have negative beliefs about yourself, this negativity takes your body energy into a downward spiral, and creates stress hormones and chemicals that flood throughout the body.

It stands to reason when your energies are high and you feel good about your life, your immune system is boosted, keeping you healthy and further enhancing the good feelings about yourself. When you are in a down space, you feel more negativity and as a consequence your immune system's defense system releases more stress chemicals, opening your body to imbalance and more stress. On a long-term basis this can lead to burnout, adrenal fatigue, and a body that is weakened, which expresses itself as dis-ease.

Your Outer World and Stress

Over the last 40 years the world has become more and more stressful to inhabit. It has become like a super-highway, with more and more information being shared at increasing speeds. With the advent of Facebook, Twitter, and other social media outlets, there is so much more for you to keep up with. Your world is forever busy.

In the modern world, you are constantly bombarded with visions of war-torn countries, poverty, disease, and starvation, and somehow you become numb to these images. You live in a world of social hypnosis in which you no longer recognize what is your truth.

Your Physical Environment and Stress

The effect of electromagnetic radiation or e-smog being created with all the new technology over the last 40 years is increasing daily. You live in a concrete jungle. You get affected by phone towers. You often work in air-conditioned buildings. More and more housing and concrete structures are being developed.

Chemtrails assault the airways, and pollution is rife. Forests are being cut down and natural environments are being debased by mining and gas exploration, and the chemicals being used filter into the natural water table.

Household products are filled with chemicals to keep us "germ free," but they create enormous damage to your body system with the absorption and ingesting of airborne chemicals.

The water you drink has different chemicals added to it and is no longer natural water. Toothpaste contains fluoride. Many scientific tests have been run to show that the water tables are depositories for the release of these chemicals and also medications that are released from the body.

Your Physical Health and Stress

Farmed fish and animals are fed hormones and genetically modified produce. Food is no longer natural; it is sprayed with numerous pesticides. Fast food and genetically modified engineered crops reduce the digestion to work on a minimum scale, so the daily nutritional requirement from food is no longer available in order to create a healthy body. Sugar is a big culprit in dis-ease, and many products contain artificial sweeteners that are a cause of rising obesity levels.

Some bathroom products, such as shampoos, soaps, and personal hygiene products, contain xenoestrogens. Xenoestrogens are man-made compounds that mimic the effects of natural estrogens in the body. They have an effect on health and have been linked to cancer and overweight.

Your Connection to Nature, the Community, and Stress

Connection to nature seems to have been swallowed up in this crazy world of trying to achieve more material things in life. Trying to keep up with what is happening is killing communities and connection to the more valuable things in life. More and more people live in cities, neighbor hardly knows neighbor, and more people live in singular housing and not in family units. The stress of non-connection is being compounded. It is important to recognize that one of the most primal instincts of humanity is to *belong*.

Overall Stress and its Ramifications

This is not a pretty picture, and it is vital that all the elements of stress are recognized. Not only do you have the effect of the mental and emotional aspects of yourself, but you also have the various added physical and environmental bombardment of your body. It is no wonder levels of stress and illness are increasing.

Added to this, is in today's society, generally the meaning and purpose of life and why you are here have been eroded and forgotten. The relevance of how to live as an ultimate human or a spirit with a human body is no longer of importance. The world is controlled by big business and profits; squashed in the middle, the consumer is trying to survive.

My understanding that while you are bombarded with all things physical, the real nature of dis-ease comes from the lack of connection to yourself on a spiritual basis and your source energy and true meaning. The majority of the population seems to be further removed from this principle with all the unhealthy distractions in the world.

So when you are not surrounded by what is your beauty, your spirit hangs low, your heart closes, and your love for yourself and others disappears. You get distracted by the busy-ness of life and the abundant mental chatter, emotional distress appears, and hence you manifest dis-ease. When any kind of stress—whether it be physical, mental, emotional, or spiritual—is not handled in the correct context, it keeps reappearing like a bad penny.

As a child I spent most of my days out in the fields or climbing trees. I communed with nature on a daily basis; it taught me how to honor this world. I learned how to be in tune with the earth and its inhabitants, and respect their place in the order of things. I sat in awe of colorful butter-flies, spiderwebs being woven with the light shining through them, and bathing in the splendid colors of nature. It made my heart sing.

There are many ways to handle dis-ease and stress—and I don't mean by going to a doctor for a pill! Most doctors only treat symptoms! It's time to go to the root of the problem.

It takes a deep personal journey or quest and commitment to change your life; heal and rejuvenate yourself back to a level of optimal health on all levels. Mental, emotional, physical and spiritual—all these levels need to be addressed.

It is time for the world to stand up and handle this situation head-on. The way to do this is for all of us individually to take the necessary steps to heal so a better world can be created. It is time to dig deep for the answers, where only lasting change and healing can take place for the benefit of the planet and its inhabitants at large, so you can come together with your soul family that supports and nurtures you and, in turn, create sustainable communities.

A hypothesis: If at the very core you were feeling deep peace and loving yourself and others unconditionally, then the ramifications of dis-ease and distress would probably not be so rampant and, I would suggest, would disappear.

Note to the World:

The frequency of pure love is healing, so when we love ourselves unconditionally we heal!

Chapter 3

What Takes You off Your Journey?

Ego overview

"The wound is where the light enters you."

~ *Rumi*

As you saw in the previous chapter, stress plays a big part in your being settled in your own skin and the life that you lead. You will discover in the chapters ahead other things that stand in the way of your true self and that take you off your path. Briefly, they are: your family history and upbringing, your societal influences, your thoughts, your unhealthy beliefs, your destructive decisions, your attitudes, your fears, your emotions, your patterns of behaviors and habits, and your conflicting values. What is this all about? How does it happen like this? Does anything hold it in place?

Understand that you are not your mind—that incessant babble of what goes on in your head of thoughts, beliefs, decisions, fears, emotions, and attitudes or your patterns of behaviors and habits. These are aspects of your conscious mind or your personality that have been adopted for you to operate safely through life.

Your journey along this path is to identify less and become detached from your personality. The key is to rise above it. Your mind is a tool and no more. You do this by observing what is going on with your awareness, and by becoming more conscious of your limitations and patterns of behaviors that you keep you stuck.

You are like a book. Your personality is like a mask, or a book cover, and it is what the outside world sees. The inside of the book is the richness of what you have hidden from the world.

Your Personal Ego

Your personality, which I call the ego, is not your true self. It is your separated self, which is an illusion. It is motivated by the pain pleasure principle. You either run away from your pain or run toward your pleasure.

When you are controlled by your ego, you are either worrying about what has happened in the past (which you cannot change, as it has already happened; you can only change your response to it) or you are concerned about the future (which is yet to happen and, again, over which you have no control).

Both directions prevent you being here now, and you miss the richness of the moment. It has gone. So don't let yourself be distracted by the continual mind chatter. Trust that you will have all you need at the moment, as life creates itself moment by moment. As Eckhart Tolle states, *"There is no pain in the present moment!"*

Remember you are part of the universal energy source, which is connected to all things.

While your true nature is the essence of self, you spend much time in the third-dimensional world, being controlled by your ego or personality. Your ego is like sand; it is rough and brings you the lessons and the friction to make you grow. Your essence is the sweetness of life, which gives you the ability to create and experience beauty, love, and joy.

According to Freud's psychoanalytic theory of the personality, the personality is composed of three elements, known as the id, the ego, and the superego, they work together to create complex human behaviors.

The **id** is driven by the *pleasure principle*, which strives for immediate gratification of all desires, wants, and needs. Picture a baby wanting his or her needs met immediately.

The **ego** is the component of personality that is responsible for dealing with reality. According to Freud, the ego develops from the id and ensures that the impulses of the id can be expressed in a manner acceptable in the real world.

The **superego** is the last component of personality to develop, around age 5. As Freud stated, the superego is the aspect of personality that holds all of your internalized moral standards and ideals that you acquire from both parents and society—your sense of right and wrong. From these guidelines you make judgments and criticisms of yourself and project them onto others.

You arrive on this planet in part with your wonderful childlike innocence, with little experience in life at such an early age to gain any wisdom. Ego is given to you as a useful tool to learn about life and experience for a time.

The ego is your teacher. It is in place to give you experiences in life regarding what is appropriate or not. Think of yourself as a child. When you place your hand onto something hot on the stove, you soon learn that you will burn and hurt yourself if you continue to do this.

Your ego allows you to develop and hone your skills to learn about life. For a while this is an essential part of your natural development. While it is important during your childhood for this learning to take place, at some point in time your essence gets largely suppressed and the ego, not wanting to lose its identity, takes over and becomes the boss. Welcome to the superego taking over.

You lose sight of the real picture and become immersed in ego gratification. Your balance in life and coming from a higher perspective of what is going on is lost. As this happens your deeper connection to the more spiritual aspect of you slowly is eroded.

This is played out by creating division and duality in the world. You divide between male and female, the left and right sides of the brain, different nations and skin colors and religions. This keeps the conflict and illusion alive.

As an adult the purpose of identifying and exploring the different parts of your personality—your patterns, beliefs, and behaviors; your hurts and fears; and what makes you tick in that sense—is vital. By learning about these aspects of yourself and using tools to take back control, you start to undo the ego. This makes you stronger and ultimately will set you free to experience yourself in your truth. It will serve you well!

It is quite normal for us to be trained in the following adage of **Do, Be, Have.** We are led to believe that having something first like the money or the car is necessary before you can start doing what you want, which then allows you to be who you want to be. Following this way, you never get out of the starting gate. You will never be the person you want to be if you have to wait. It is called the "wanna be" syndrome!

This is not your true state; you are a divine being, in a state of being-ness.

Herein lies the secret!

It is the other way around. It goes more like this: **Be, Do, Have.** Be the person you truly are through an open heart and the love you are. This will lead you into being able to accomplish what you want to do, resulting in rewarding you with a magical life.

Do, Be, Have comes from a state of separation, duality, and doing-ness. **Be, Do, Have** is based on oneness of spirit and a state of being-ness. This is a big difference! Unfortunately the norm for society comes from **Do, Be, Have**, and it has led to an unbalanced society.

The Collective Ego

Not only is your own ego at work, you are also being subtly affected by the collective ego. Many hours are spent in activities in which you are influenced in your working life in the corporate arena, politics and government, different religious groups, and your communities.

As David Wilcock's states, *"Life on Earth is a vast illusion, structured for the explicit purpose of spiritual evolution for all its participants. We have large amounts of time to learn our lessons—across many lifetimes—while living in very significant amnesia of our greater Identity."*

With the introduction of social media and the Internet, the world has become very small. The reporting of news and happenings around the world is available 24/7 at a touch of a button. Advertising abounds in magazines, in your communities, on the Net, through entertainment, and on TV.

Most of the Western and corporate world today encourages and rewards material gain with little importance put on the spiritual side of your nature. Some people have the illusion that you are your possessions, your job, your car, your latest holiday, your house, and your status in the world. This is not so; these are just personality identities or aspects of your ego that you wear as masks. This is the **Do, Be, Have** syndrome in full action.

Society is influenced by these collective planetary energies, which are speeding up. Countries across the world are rising from a deep slumber, and humanity is raising its voice and being heard. They want something different. The world is stirring and waking up. It has been a long time in the semi-light of truth.

Gradually more light is filtering through, and glimpses of living a better way are leaking through the veils as the populace stirs. You can see looking around people wanting to live differently.

There are lessons the world is being given on a collective basis that require change for us to thrive. For instance, disasters like Hurricane Katrina and oil spills speak of the need to seriously look at how energy systems are fueled.

You only have to view the world's different indigenous cultures and inhabitants for examples of their spirit connection to nature, and the love and honoring of the interconnectedness of all living things. It shows how the world could live another way by taking care of the earth, and protecting the environment and its beauty. By following your own path and journey you are supporting this awakening.

Your Evolutionary Journey

"For things to change first I must change" is a statement used in the Money and You series of workshops. Are you ready to take the steps for your change? Are you ready to do what it takes?

People are breaking through their illusions. It is a very exciting time to be alive, sitting on the cliff ready to fly, with wings outstretched to take off.

This time in history is an invitation to open up and discover your deeper self. It is time for the emergence of your essence, like the blossoming of a beautiful flower or a radiant butterfly emerging from the chrysalis, ready for full flight, changing from ego to your true expression.

You are a spirit in human form, here to expand your awareness and connect with your soul to play, create and have fun, and **be** true to the divine essence of who you are.

Remember: Live a life worth living by living from the inside out. You are whom you have been waiting for!

Section Two

Digging Deep and Delving into Your Past History

Chapter 4

What Stands in Your way of Being at Peace?

Your fears, beliefs, emotions, decisions, attitudes, and mind-sets

"One cannot be prepared for something
while secretly believing it will not happen."

~ Nelson Mandela

Early-childhood experiences can have a profound effect on you as you grow up and on your adult life. The decisions made about your early experiences can be colored by fear reactions such as anger, separation, and loss felt by the body.

Beliefs are then formed by the ego. That creates the base platform of how you live your life in the future. Life is then lived from a contracted perspective as you limit your horizon. This is what stands in the way of your being at peace—your sacred wounds, and everyone carries them.

Everything in life is in relationship to everything else, so experience comes from seeing and understanding yourself from this perspective. There is no other way to perceive.

Sometimes you fail to see the bigger picture and only see certain parts of your life; you are blind to different aspects. To achieve a sense of peace

33

and space it is advantageous to live in a broader way, which requires you to view your life from a higher perspective.

Picture an eagle soaring in the sky above, and imagine what they see from so high up in the sky. An eagle is able to see so much more from up there. You, too, need to work toward that way of being, rather than being stuck on the ground!

The world is full of information; you receive it constantly, second by second. You filter this new data though your brain, relative to previously stored information, so you automatically respond or react.

It is a natural phenomenon that you, as a child, made decisions based on responses to experiences, and you live your life in a certain way. You develop and adopt beliefs to support these decisions, which are subjective and are upheld by emotions based on love or fear. This, in turn, creates your values, your attitudes, and your habits to handle the negativity, which governs the way you turn up in the world in your truth. These can be full of limitations and constrictions as though you are inside the box—or, you could even say, in your comfort zone.

The decisions you make and the beliefs you adopt are based on your core fears or separation. These dominate you in all that you do and how you express yourselves. This can be unnerving at the best of times, as often you are unconscious of what is driving you.

This starts in the early years when you are a child—a formative time, when impressions are made easily. You experience painful events, see your parents arguing, maybe are frightened by being left alone by yourself, are not nurtured with love or kindness, are shocked by something, or experience the death of someone dear to you. Generally at school you were not allowed to express your natural self, and you may have been bullied.

Your parents also have their own hurts and patterns of behaviors, and decisions they have made in the past. Often these patterns are unresolved and become triggers for behaviors from which they operate in full force. For instance, a parent might have loved another and still stayed in the marriage for the sake of the children. This could have resulted in him or her becoming embittered and unhappy.

You take this history on as yours, and this leads you into decisions and behaviors about how to be. Your patterns are set, based on not only your own experiences but those of a genetic nature, too!

Can you recognize that you suppress the innate expression of who you are in order to conform, be accepted, fit in, and belong?

The pattern of how to operate is now established through creating a set of behaviors and memories. The body, through the nervous system, learns to react from this template and uses it for all future incoming information. It is like putting an instruction into the operating system of a computer. Unless you manually change it, it will still obey these instructions. Your brain becomes wired with these instructions and patterns.

At this stage you operate from a disassociated space, are disconnected from your soul, and go along in life half asleep. Each time you have a similar experience it goes into the storage bank, stacking on top of the other cellular memories already stored in your subconscious.

Eventually the dam bursts; you are unable to do this—to be who you are not—anymore. You become emotionally like a seesaw, unbalanced in your thoughts and actions, resulting in you being unable to cope with life in general. It's similar to swimming in the swamp with the crocodiles, with stress rearing its ugly head!

In kinesiology we describe this as **your negative fear spiral,** which takes your energy vibration downward.

A fact happens; a fear is felt. You now have the memory of the event tainted by the fear, you make a decision or adopt a belief, which is stored in your cellular system, and you then lock that into position. Your response is to feel hurt, angry, sad, or fearful.

Each time a similar feeling event takes place, you refer to the original feeling and what has already transpired, making the assumption that this is how life is. Your life is then governed by past events and projected out to the future. This pattern then becomes the norm.

An example of this is a small child who witnesses her parents having an argument with raised, angry voices. She is frightened and terrified about what is happening. She does not understand, feels helpless, and doesn't know how to stop the situation. It is so different from her normal experience of her parents' relationship.

She observes the fact of the fight, reacts with feelings of fear and terror, and experiences helplessness in the situation. This memory is now locked into her cellular memory. This pattern can be compounded if she experiences more of the same.

Rather than being in the present moment, you come from your history. A major part of unraveling your story is to identify your core fears, destructive decisions, and unhealthy beliefs, mind-sets, and major emotions that control you. Below I explain each of these areas to allow you to identify more of your story. Before we go there, though, I would like you to try an experiment.

Think of something that makes you feel very happy. It may be a walk on the beach or it may seeing your children play. Close your eyes, take deep breath, and get in touch with that feeling. How does your energy feel? Has it gone up a notch or two? Open your eyes.

Now, think of something that makes you sad or angry, like a sad movie or something that you are upset about. Close your eyes and take deep breath. Really feel the experience. How do you feel now? Has your energy dropped down?

Return your attention to the good feeling you had before you read on!

This brief experiment shows you how positive and negative thoughts can affect the way you feel very quickly, from love to fear, or fear to love; it is instantaneous. The wonderful thing about this small experiment is it shows you how you can control your energy output, just by changing your thinking. You always have a choice.

Peace is a state of being—a state of inner harmony that you cannot chase. A state of being is the result of the love you feel for yourself and how you feel inside. It is you at your core. While something may make you feel happy, the only way to find that deep inner sense of joy and peace is inside you. It is a daily journey moment by moment.

The Start of Your Journey of Discovery

This is the start of your journey of discovery, where you will commence your inquiry into your past and start to collect information about your story, your background, your beliefs, the decisions that you have taken that has stopped you going forward, and your deepest fears and trepidations. In future chapters you will be filling out this story, and by the end of the book, you will have a very comprehensive history of your life and a new pathway leading you toward an **adventure for your soul**—a lifetime journey!

Please ensure that you have a journal you would like to write in or special paper, pens, and colored pens, maybe some Post-It notes, lots of water, and soothing music if you would like.

Choose a place that is supportive to you when doing this work, and ensure that you do this when you can be undisturbed. Are you ready to go on journey of a lifetime? Thank yourself for getting to this point and taking the plunge!

Fears

Fears are illusions of the mind that you create about what has happened to you in the past and, based on that, what may happen to you in the future. Fears are a form of threat or a response from outside events that gives you memories, which you store in your subconscious mind.

They are based on the pain pleasure principle of childhood. Know that fears are not real or tangible. They are often hidden. They hamper your expansion and keep you stuck, limiting and holding you back while taking your energy levels on a downward spiral.

Your everyday fears can vary from not being happy or finding your place in life, to finding the relationship you want, to having enough money to pay the bills, to questions like "Will my child be safe and grow up okay?" Adding to that any basic fears you may have of, say, heights, spiders, being on your own, and physical activities can make life confronting.

Your remedy is often to deny and run away from these feelings, getting involved with activities that take you away from the threats. You may hear yourself lament, "Where are the joy and peace I am so looking for?"

While you are affected by your own personal fears, understand there are also universal or collective fears that permeate the air around you. You can pick these up from your environment, naturally absorbing them unknowingly.

As you are all one and interconnected, it is easy to see how you can be at the effect of such happenings and carry this with you through your daily life. It is like a vicious circle: The more you dwell on these happenings, the more your energy spirals downward. I have listed the three major collective or universal fears here.

The Three Universal Fears

Universal fear is in the energy of the collective around you that you absorb. It has a penetrating effect when your personal vibration is low. The fear of abandonment and separation, the fear of being not worthy or good enough, and the fear of intimacy, surrender, and trust, are at the foundation of what we experience as collective fear. Be aware of this, as it clouds your judgment of your own situation.

These energies are emitted from such situations of a national concern that are reported in the media or that other people focus on, such as terrorist attacks, shortage of oil, wars, cancer, poverty, sickness, cruelty, and financial crises. These affect you at a very deep vibrational level, and on top of them you build your own personal fears, leading you with the feeling of being open to attack, vulnerable, and unsafe.

Gregg Braden states in his book *Walking between the Worlds* that we have been historically plugged into a fear-based collective energy field for 200,000 years. When we come into this world as a blank slate, we are given an electrical antenna that plugs into the beliefs, joys, and fears of those who have come before us. So we live life through the lens and perceptions of others, until we consciously choose to do differently. Studies show that this is experienced across each culture and ethnic background.

Plugging into these three universal fields keeps the promise that what you bring into your life will be what you most fear through the areas of relationships, careers, and friendships, so you are unable to find healing and balance in your lives.

1. Fear of Abandonment and Separation

In your deepest memories there is a feeling that you came to this world, and were left and forgotten. You feel alone. This memory runs so deep you no longer register with the reason, but the electrical charge is still there.

You act this out by creating relationships, career opportunities, and friendships that mirror these fears back to you. You feel devastated when they fail your expectations and you get left behind, or maybe you choose to leave first and sabotage the situation so you protect yourself from experiencing the pain of the abandonment and separation.

As you go through the following sections, write down what you recognize to be true for you in your journal, and write anything in your life that relates to your life so far.

2. Fear of Being Not Worthy or Good Enough

This relates to issues of low self-esteem. You question your own value and worth.

You mirror your fears by creating relationships that match your expected beliefs of your low self-esteem and stay in those relationships unnecessarily. You stay in your job, which you are not enjoying, as you do feel worthy of getting a job you like. You put up with friends you don't enjoy, or who do not support and nurture you.

You can have the experience of walking into a room and being concerned that everyone is looking at you and judging you. You compare yourself with others. You feel guilty about things in your life. Your life matches up to your feelings of not being worthy or good enough.

3. Fear of Intimacy, Surrender, and Trust

Ask yourself these questions: *Do you implicitly trust life? Do you feel safe and secure living in this world, especially today? Do you get concerned when you say goodbye to a loved one, and have a concern at the back of your mind that something may happen and it will be the last time you see him or her?*

Your world will be mirrored back to you through this lack of trust. It will be hard for you to surrender and trust in life and the process of flow, as you will want control of it. Intimacy issues will abound, and being open-hearted and vulnerable will be a test.

There are other fears, such as rejection, scarcity, change, failure, meaninglessness, shame, powerlessness, loss, and vulnerability. These you can list under the above categories as sub-fears.

It's okay if you've experienced these fears for yourself; they are common. Later I'll give you some exercises to help you understand and be able to handle them.

Task: Label this part of your journal the Discovery section. As you read through the universal fears write down in the Discovery section of your journal the one that seems to resonate the most, and any other thoughts, events, or people that seem pertinent to this. If more than one rings a bell, write them down, too. We are starting to capture a picture of your life.

Negative Emotions

All negative emotions are reflective of fear, anger, lust, grief, apathy, and shame are major fears, and have many sub-groups under them. For example, you may recognize some of these, which manifest in various behaviors and attitudes.

Anger: Impatience, frustration, resentment, hate, antagonism, meanness, self-destruction, and narrow-mindedness.

Lust: Jealousy, greed, possessiveness, denial, demanding, manipulation, recklessness, compulsion, and addiction.

Fear itself: Insecurity, self-doubt, anxiety, mistrust, defensiveness, panic, worry, dread, withdrawal, suspicion, nervousness, terror, paralysis, and fear of being punished.

Grief: Sadness, unhappiness, guilt, and feeling hurt, rejected, neglected, inferior, and betrayed.

Apathy: Worthlessness, insignificance, depression, helplessness, hopelessness, despair, devastation, discouragement, and feeling too exhausted.

Shame: Humiliation, disgrace, dishonor, embarrassment, inadequacy, misery, feeling not welcomed, and feeling inferior.

There are many, more—too many to list. In fact, you can create an A–Z of negative emotions and be very surprised at how many there are! In my work and my own personal experience of healing, it is advisable to be exact in recognizing the word or words that ring a bell in specific situations.

As we have discovered, there are two major emotional energies: *love* or *fear*. What you feel activates certain neurotransmitters in the brain that send a signal to the nervous system, and your body will experience the up feeling of love or the down feeling of fear, affecting your immune system and stress response. Love is the frequency that heals and spreads through the body and supports the immune system of the body. Fear does the opposite.

I like to reframe the word *fear* as a call for love. It helps seeing any fear in a kinder light and therefore is easier to face, accept, and overcome.

Task: As you read through the negative emotions above, in the Discovery section of your journal, write down the categories that resonate for you and any other words that are listed in that category that ring a bell, too. Add anything that seems pertinent to this, such as people, events, and situations you may experience.

Destructive Decisions, Unhealthy Beliefs, Attitudes, and Mind-Sets

In the negative fear spiral model explored above, a fear is felt that results in a bodily response you experience. You make a certain decision to ensure your safety and protection.

Ensuring a decision holds fast, you adopt beliefs that support the decision. For instance, you have a bodily response of fear; your ego makes a mental decision, which gets supported by an emotional belief that installs this process further.

Here's an example. You fall out of a tree and feel fear, your ego makes the decision that it is not safe to do anything on your own, and your emotional response in the form of a belief may be "I am hopeless; I cannot do things on my own" or "I am frightened to do anything on my own; I will get hurt unless there is someone to support me."

Destructive Decisions

In the formative years of childhood, a decision is made from a mental perspective by the ego, resulting from feeling fear and emotion that are experienced and felt. The decision is often irrational, but at the time keeps the child safe.

A small child does not have the total understanding of what is really happening in the world, and from that illogical space makes a decision and sets it in concrete about how it is going to be and how this will control his or her world in the future.

The problem here is that in your adult life you are governed by decisions you make to protect you. It takes control of you at a level that is sometimes absurd, and your experiences of life can be stunted. While a decision made as a child may have been appropriate, the question remains: Is the decision appropriate for adulthood? Mostly no, as it limits and suppresses your ability to shine in what and who you are and it affects the way you live.

> **Task:** As you read through the destructive decisions information, in your journal write down any decisions you have made that stop you from moving forward. Add to this anything that seems pertinent, including people, events, and situations you may have experienced. For example: "I am not safe, so I cannot go on holiday on my own"; "I have no particular talents, so I am not bright"; "I can't do, be, or have something because...."

Unhealthy Beliefs

Beliefs can be many and varied: good ones and not-so-good ones. Unhealthy beliefs are the ones that keep you small, do not serve you, and emotionally cause stress to the body.

Beliefs are "I'm worthless," "I'm helpless and can't do it on my own," "I am not safe," "I'm not good enough," "I'm lonely," "Something bad will happen to me," "People leave me," or "I'm so alone."

It is important to become aware of which ones are prevalent for you. Everyone has these sorts of beliefs until there is recognition of what is going on and a decision can be made to take action toward identifying and releasing them consciously.

Task: As you read through the unhealthy beliefs information, in your journal write down any unhealthy beliefs you carry that you are becoming aware of. Add to this anything that seems pertinent, including people, events, and situations you may have experienced.

Attitudes

When you adopt attitudes of which you are not aware, your life has a habit of getting stuck and does not flow. I call these blind spots; they get in the way of our natural essence. These include:

- **Resistance:** Not going with the flow by resisting what is based on your fears and beliefs.

- **Limitations:** Stunting your natural abilities and expression by living inside your box.

- **Projection:** Projecting your fears and beliefs onto others rather than taking responsibility.

- **Self-talk:** Talking to yourself in a destructive manner; lowering your vibrational frequency.

- **Control:** Having to have too much control and not going with the flow.

- **Attention:** Putting your attention on the glass half empty and what doesn't work for you.

- **Avoidance:** Avoiding your truth; distracting yourself away from what needs your attention and action.

- **Denial:** Believing in an illusion about the truth of your life, putting your head in the sand.

- **Boundaries:** Unhealthy or lack of boundaries, and merging with others energies.

- **Surrogation:** Taking on others' energies and claiming them to be yours.

- **Conscious conflict:** Living out something you don't believe in for fear of reprisal.

Task: Go through the above list and write down the attitudes that you carry and act out that have up until now supported you through your life. Write down any insights you get about your relationships and events in your life where you have played or do play this out.

Mind-Sets

This sets in motion you establishing different mind-sets of locking in the beliefs and fears, for example, called the "what if?" syndrome: "What if I wasn't afraid of? I would…"; "What if I lost my job? What will happen to me?"; "What if I was more beautiful?"; "What if I get sick? What will I do?"; "What if I can't do…?"; "What if something unforeseen happens to stop me…?"; "What if my partner left me? What would I do?"

They all seem to come from the "what if?" syndrome and keep us stuck, worried, and awake at night. It is an exhausting state to live in and diminishes our energy and health. Shel Silverstein wrote a poem about this very issue called "Whatif."

Task: As you read through the mind-sets section, write down all of the "what ifs?" of which you are cognizant. Add to this anything that seems pertinent, such as people, events, and situations you may have experienced.

Take a deep breath and congratulate yourself on having started this journey.

You may well be asking or thinking, "Will I ever get out of the rabbit hole that I have created? Will this ever stop? Will I ever make sense of it all? Will I ever have a hope of finding my way through this maze?"

Yes. You do so by being aware of how and what you think, how you behave, how you feel about yourself and your world around you, how you see yourself in your own image, and how you look after, nurture, and love yourself. It is a case of not learning or searching for something else or someone else; it is remembering who you really are—pure love, a beautiful expression of the divine.

How you manage these fears, destructive decisions, unhealthy emotions, attitudes, and mind-sets is a personal choice. Remember: These are just different aspects of yourself that come from your early childhood to keep you safe, and they do affect what is important to you.

The bottom line here is to understand that the ultimate result of this negative way of being creates conflicts among your values and reflects in the way you are in your life. Clarity disappears and confusion reigns; it's a way in which self-sabotage happens.

You either will come from a place of victimization and a "poor me" attitude, and believe that they cannot be changed and allow them to control you—or you can have the intention that you will take one step at a time with different techniques and tools to shift your perspective of your situation, and heal your life by taking on new concrete philosophies and ground rules.

Again, I want to reiterate these are only signposts that you have cre-ated along the way in your life, and it is your **choice** to make the neces-sary steps to move beyond them. They are not you or fixed for life. How-ever, these fears, decisions, beliefs, emotions, attitudes, and mind-sets are so often insidious. You claim them as yours by making them into habits, and, like smoking, they can be hard to give up and release!

The ultimate choice is yours. Make **a decision and a commitment to yourself.** A decision and commitment to this type of living do not serve or support you to be the glorious divine human you were born to be. Your potential is waiting in the wings to be expressed. Bring out your core essence and shine your diamond.

***

We have started the first phase of collecting information of your life history. Your next step is to discover all the different ways in which you block your peace. You will come back to this information later when you pull all the information together.

In the next chapter you will go into depth into the different contexts of your life. I have designed this exercise to be done over an 11-day period, allowing for less stress and time for contemplation, and allowing your soul to come up with information from your subconscious that is buried deeper that is not necessarily available to you on a conscious basis. Read on!

Chapter 5

Identifying the Pain and Challenges of Your Life

The contexts of your life

"In the moments of your greatest Pain,
lies the opportunity for the greatest growth."

~ *Chao Kee Lim*

The work I do brings me in touch with people who are in pain. It has been difficult for them to have a sense of peace and fulfillment, and to be themselves and generally lead a rich and rewarding life.

Living today feels more harried, especially in these chaotic times. It requires a different skill set of strength and purpose about your journey through life.

Nowadays you are affected by so many external energies that were not apparent 40 years ago. Children spend more time in front of the TV and play more computer games than you ever did. At that time, computers were not around on a personal scale.

The use of modern gadgets and mobile phones is epidemic and is putting out an ever-increasing amount of electromagnetic radiation. You are living and working in these environments on a daily basis, surrounded by this invisible e-smog.

More and more people are living in concrete field cities with little nature and becoming ungrounded. On top of this you ingest genetically modified food and junk food. It seems you have less personal time available; your working life turns out to be one mad rush, and generally you're trying to keep up with the frenetic changes that constantly appear. Under these circumstances it is possible that you have lost connection with yourself and your purpose for being here. This puts you under enormous stress and strain, and is a source of possible health issues.

So learning how to *be* in this world requires a different set of values, mind-set, behaviors, and attitudes. Only you can do this; it is a solo journey, and possibly that can be the scariest part especially from an ego perspective. However, know this: You are not alone on this journey. Everyone has a choice to go down this road if they want inner peace, and many are doing this.

Pain is given to you so you can recognize something is not right in your world; it is a signal from your innate knowing to wake up. It gives you an indication that there is something to understand and comprehend on a deeper level. Pain is just getting your attention; it's saying, "Hi. Look at me." It's a little bit like a naughty child saying, "Notice me! I need your attention! I am hurting!"

In this chapter you will start finding and acknowledging the source of your pain and what is going on. I will give you a comprehensive picture of what is happening.

Let us do that: Let us identify your pain!

Remember that once you have acknowledged what the picture looks like, it is easier to go forward. So please be as honest as you can with yourself. Denial won't work here. You may even need a tissue box, and that's okay (better out than in!). You will be doing great work!

Here are the areas that we are going to cover in detail:

- **Intimate relationships:** your love life, partnerships, and marriages.

- **Self-recognition:** how you see yourself in the world.

- **Family and health:** your background history and state of health.

- **Prosperity, abundance, and fortunate blessings:** how and what you manifest in life.

- **Creativity and your inner child:** your creativity and childlike playfulness.

- **Career and your life path:** your passions and talents expressed through your work.

- **Inner knowledge and intuition:** how well you know you and use your intuition.

- **Support, helpful friends, and fun:** the support and fun you experience.

- **Unity:** your light vibration, balance, energy levels, and general flow.

The Contexts of Your Life

Prosperity, Abundance and Fortunate Blessings	Self-Recognition	Intimate Relationships
Family and Health	Unity	Creativity and Your Inner Child
Inner Knowledge and Intuition	Career and Your Life Path	Support, Helpful Friends, and Fun

All of these areas are inter-connected. However, eight pair up and have a direct influence by reflecting and supporting each other:

1. **Intimate relationships–Support, helpful friends, and fun.**

2. **Self-recognition–Career and life path.**

3. **Family and health–Prosperity, abundance, and fortunate blessings.**

4. **Creativity and children–Inner knowledge and intuition.**

Let's get started.

Find a comfortable chair; sit in a space that is pleasing to your senses and supports you. Remember to keep breathing and ensure you are not disturbed. Have water handy (the brain can get very tired if not hydrated!) and maybe play some soothing music.

This exercise is designed to be completed over an 11-day period (one section a day). Using your special journal, which you have already started, continue doing freeform writing for exploration. When this is done over a period of time, the subconscious mind gets alerted about other information to release that is buried at a deeper level.

Treat this part of the process with respect. Preferably, no mind chatter or self-judgment. Have a "no excuses" mind-set. Be kind to yourself. It is your life I am talking about, and to me **that is important.**

As you go through each area, I will give you different prompts. With each category there are eight tasks designed to give you a current overview. It follows this format:

1. A brief description of the category, noting your "ouch" statements.

2. The upside and downside of each area where you are blocking or flowing.

3. The key or mind-set to adopt that takes you through the maze.

4. Three tasks designed for you to discover your truths.

5. The costs and consequences of you not having what you want now, one year from now, and five years from now.

6. Your highlights, wins, and contributions, and what has been good for you.

7. What the benefits of you having this would be now, one year from now, and five years from now.

8. One step that you will commit to and action to start changing this area of your life.

Put some fun into this exercise! Be as light as you can, use different colored pens, and even draw symbols and pictures! It is **an adventure of the soul.** Treat it with curiosity.

In the next chapter, after you have completed Day 11, covering all the different areas, I will give you instructions on how to pull it all together and where you go from there.

Day 1: Intimate Relationships

There is one certainty: Everyone at some time has had intimate relationships. Your relationships with others, especially your loved ones, offer a wonderful opportunity to grow. I liken it to flowers or plants growing; they need friction—something to push or resist against—so they can move past the obstacle of the earth and become that beautiful flower. This can wear you down without the right tools to manage it.

Downside: Emotional roller coaster, feeling loss and betrayal
Upside: Growth, honesty, and intimacy
Keys: Vulnerability and surrender

How do you feel about your intimate relationships? Read aloud all the statements in the different categories. Even if your situation is different, do any of them hit the spot? Write down the ones that give you the strongest feeling response with an emotional charge.

For example:

If you are single: You cannot find the right person. When you were in a relationship it was never the right one. You cannot trust anyone to be that close to you. You were let down and betrayed. The right one will never come along. You never know where you stand in the dating scene.

If you have just ended a relationship: You don't want to go home after work and face an empty house. You have felt lonely without someone to share your life with. You have the thought of there never being another one you could love as much. You feel guilty about what happened and you blame yourself. You want revenge on the other party as you feel so hurt.

If you are in a relationship or married: You don't feel heard or understood by your significant other. If you say the wrong thing explosions happen and your partner snaps. You squirm in the presence of your partner and feel judged. You don't feel nourished or cherished in the way you would like. There are things you would like to change in your relationship and you don't have the courage to broach the subject.

Generally: You avoid the subject of relationships. Relationship dreams and expectations have flown out the window and you wake up sad each day. You don't feel welcome by the opposite sex. Your relationships leave you feeling unimportant and insignificant. You feel judged. Anything you do isn't okay. Betrayal is hard to get over. You feel unlovable and get rejected. Sex has gone out the window.

Tasks:

After the statements that you have already noted, write nonstop about your personal relationship experiences: how it really feels to you; what has happened; the concerns you have. Remember: This is crunch time. Be honest with yourself. The key is to keep the pen moving.

Write down the **costs and consequences** to you personally of not having the relationship in your life you want. Where are you stuck? What do you want in your life that you don't have? What is the cost of this now? What will the cost be a year from now? Five years from now? Thank you for your honesty!

On the next page of your journal, list what have been the *highlights* in your relationships—what has worked for you in relationships and why. Do you have any proud moments? What are the good memories?

Now write down what would be the **benefits and rewards** of having the relationship of your dreams. How would you be different in your life? How would it look? How would you feel? If you were to release and let go of these reasons of the costs and consequences, how would it improve your life?

What freedom would that give you? What would that allow you to do now, in one year, and five years from now? What's the importance of this? How committed are you? On a scale of one to 10 (one being the lowest), how committed are you to these improvements?

Commitment: Write down one action you will commit to take in how you will approach and experience relationships.

Suggested Ideas: Listen more and ask more questions. Identify your boundaries. Breathe more. Is there anything else that comes to mind?

Day 2: Self-Recognition

You all need to shine in your own unique way. The life path you have led so far—the experiences of pain, hurt, and traumas you have experienced along the way—sometimes have led you not to believe and trust in your innate gifts and talents. You are here to express these and, in so doing, your inner beauty graciously flowers. You are all unique. None of us is the same. You all have something special that is your thing to shine and be recognized for! When you do this, you make the world a better place, as everyone joins together in this collective energy of humanity.

> **Downside:** Low self-esteem and feeling defeated
> **Upside:** Being unique and happy to shine
>   **Keys: Your purpose, vision, and contribution**

How do you feel about self-recognition? Read aloud the statements. Which one hits the spot? Write down the ones that give you the strongest feeling response and an emotional charge.

For example:

Do you cringe at being noticed? Are you fearful of speaking on stage? Is it hard for you to find the courage to stand up and be seen? Do you feel ashamed if someone criticizes you? Are you frightened of being punished if you speak up when something isn't right in your world? Does being the center of attention make you feel vulnerable? Is sabotage your number-one enemy? When someone doesn't approve of you, do you want to hide? Maybe you don't feel worthy of being seen? Do you feel like a fraud?

> **Tasks:**
>
> After the statements that you have already noted, sit and write nonstop about how you see yourself and your experiences. How does this affect your life? Why and where are you

not shining your gifts? What is your current issue relating to your life where you felt held back? What are your worst fears? What would you like people to recognize in you? What would you like to be recognized for? What legacy would you like to leave? How do you see yourself? The key is to keep the pen moving and keep writing until you think you have covered everything.

Write down the **costs and consequences** to you personally of not having the recognition in your life you want. Where are you stuck? What do you want in your life that you don't have? What is the cost of this now, what will the cost be a year from now, and what will the cost be five years from now? Thank you for your honesty!

On your next page list the *contributions* that you make. What are you recognized for by others? What do you do well that is automatic for you? Do you have any proud moments at school or at work or in your life?

Now write down what would be the **benefits and rewards** of being recognized for whom you are. What would you do in your life if you were to step into your power, release, and let go of these reasons of the costs and consequences? How would it improve your life? What freedom would that give you? What would that allow you to do now, in one year, and five years from now? What's the importance of this? How committed are you? On a scale of one to 10 (one being the lowest), how committed are you to these improvements?

Commitment: What one action will you commit yourself to and take that will allow you to shine, be seen, and be recognized in the world?

Suggested Ideas: Write a list of your gifts and talents. Design a vision for your life. Write down your dreams. What makes your heart sing? Ask others for feedback on your gifts. What could you contribute to your family, your community, and the world?

Day 3: Family and Health

Whether you live in a family unit or you're single, you were born into a family. It's important to understand you have been impacted by your family and past generations—family traditions and values, along with beliefs, limitations, and quirks. Usually these influences are not in your conscious awareness but in subconscious patterning—patterning you don't readily see. Both emotional and physical adult health is influenced by the stresses and joys of childhood. And it's these stresses, along with decisions you've made and beliefs you hold, that can create dis-ease patterns in the body and hamper your equilibrium.

Downside: Stress, dis-ease, feelings of not belonging and limitations

Upside: Balance in life and a knowing of being true to yourself

  Family Key: Acceptance of what is and forgiveness

  Health Key: Balance and all things in moderation

Family

How do you feel about your family? Read aloud the statements. Which ones resonate and make their mark? Write down the ones that give you the strongest feeling response and an emotional charge.

For example:

Do you feel left out of the family? Were you made fun of and ridiculed as a child? Did competition abound with your siblings? Were you ever heard or recognized for you? Were you heavily controlled? It is necessary to protect yourself when around your family? Did you feel loved by your parents? Were affection and love nonexistent? Were you emotionally or physically abused? As a child were you allowed to express yourself? Did you feel smothered? Was playing the role of the black sheep the role you adopted? What other role did you play—maybe the hero, or the scapegoat? Did you feel lonely?

Tasks:

After the statements that you have already noted, sit and write nonstop about how you fit into your family of origin. What were the mood and situation like in your family? Did your parents have a happy relationship or not? Did they argue? How was the communication of the family? How did you react as a child? What are your memories from child-hood? How is being in the family in current time? Do you still feel the effect of those times? How constricted or limited did you feel, and in what way?

Write down the **costs and consequences** to you person-ally of not fitting into your family. What has this meant to you in your life? Where are you stuck? What do you want to change? What is the cost of it now? What would be the cost of this a year from now, and five years from now? Thank you for your honesty!

Go to your next page list the *good things* about your fam-ily—the fond memories that you hold and your favorite times together. Who were your favorite people and why? What was it that you liked about them? What good times do you remember having with your siblings? What did you laugh about? How do you contribute to your family? What were family celebrations like?

Now write down what would be the **benefits and rewards** to you and your family if you were to step into your true self, release, and let go of these reasons of the costs and con-sequences. How would it improve your life? What freedom would that give you? What would that allow you to do now, in one year, and five years from now? What's the importance of this? How committed are you? On a scale of one to 10 (one being the lowest), how committed are you to these improvements?

Commitment: What one action will you commit yourself to and take relating to how you can improve your relationship with your family?

Suggested Ideas: Whom do you need to forgive? Organize more contact and communication with your family. Create some social activity.

Health

What is your health like? The physical manifestations of bodily ills often come from other sources, such as emotional upsets, mental confusion, and lack of spiritual fulfillment.

Read aloud the statements. What describes you? Which ones give the response of ouch? Write down the ones that give you the strongest feeling response and have an emotional charge.

For example:

Do you feel overweight? Do you feel unattractive in your own skin? Do your clothes feel too tight and you can't button up your jeans? Do you get puffed just walking up the stairs? Do you have a skin rash? Is your digestion not working, and your plumbing could do with some help? Do you know you eat the wrong foods, but still keep doing it? Do you run out of energy throughout the day? Are you too tired to accomplish things? Are you able to exercise? Do you feel old before your time? Does your body ache? Do worry constantly or have panic attacks? Do you get too emotional and cannot control your emotions? Do you lose your temper easily? Are you always sad and crying?

Tasks:

After the statements that you have already noted, sit and write nonstop about yourself and your health. Where it is now? How do you feel? How you would like to be? What would you like to shift? What is your health history? Bad health often has its causes in other areas. Does your body hurt? Is your mind constantly active? Can you relax? Do you get uptight easily? The key is to keep the pen moving and keep writing until you think you have covered everything.

Write down the **costs and consequences** to you personally of not having the best health. What has this meant to you in your life? Where are you stuck on improving it? What has it cost you in jobs, relationships, and family life? What do you want to change? What is the cost of this now, what will the cost be a year from now, and what will the cost be five years from now? Thank you for your honesty!

On your next page list the *good things* about your body mind health. What works for you? What supports you? How do you feel? Are you fit?

Now write down what the **benefits and rewards** of having excellent health would be if you were to take control of your well-being, release, and let go of these reasons of the costs and consequences. How would it improve your life? What freedom would that give you? What would that allow you to do now, in one year, and five years from now? What's the importance of this? How committed are you? On a scale of one to 10 (one being the lowest), how committed are you to these improvements?

Commitment: What one action will you commit yourself to and take regarding the health and well-being of your body, heart, mind, and spirit?

Suggested Ideas: Organize more exercise. Plan better eating. Look at your emotional health and get professional support. Be aware of your mind chatter. Laugh more. Have more fun. Meditate and have quiet time.

Day 4: Prosperity, Abundance, and Fortunate Blessings

Many of you in your lives have experienced a lack of abundance and a flow of finances. You are not taught at school how to be proficient in this area and often were not taught at home; it is almost like you were expected to learn this through osmosis. Maybe you had parents who were not proficient themselves and therefore your role models have not been the best. Maybe you have always created enough but it runs through your fingertips or you are met with bad luck. Whatever it is, remember that abundance is a reflection of how you are on the inside.

> **Downside:** Unworthiness and lack of value in yourself
> **Upside:** Your value expressed as manifestation in the world
> **Keys: Your value and self-worth**

How do you feel about prosperity, abundance, and your blessings? Read aloud the statements. Which ones have been your patterns? Write down the ones that give you the strongest feeling response and have an emotional charge.

For example:

Do you feel out of control with money? Are you envious of others? Are you frightened to open the bills and avoid phone calls from the collectors? Does money flow through your fingers? Do you not know how to make ends meet? Does handling your financial affairs put you into overwhelm? Do you feel prosperous and feel blessed with good fortune? Do you feel un-deserving and lose everything you value, like relationships or the people you love? Is money sinful? In business, do you feel you are of value enough and cannot charge what you are worth? Do you attract bad luck and life doesn't go your way?

Tasks:

After the statements that you have already noted, write non-stop about how it has been for you and your experiences. Remember to play with a different colored pen! Write down your earliest memories of the wealth situation in your family. How did this affect you as a family, and how do you feel about it? Did you have money or not? How is your current financial situation? Are you debt free or just making ends meet? Do you have debt? This section is closely connected to your family upbringing so don't be surprised if old hurts come up; write about them. What is the situation of your abundance and prosperity right now? Have you had different periods of your life that have been different—money one day and not the next? Truthfully, where are you now?

Write down the **costs and consequences** to you personally of your money and abundance situation. What has this meant to you in your life? Where are you stuck? What do you want to change? What is the cost of this now, what will the cost be a year from now, and what will the cost be five years from now? Thank you for your honesty!

On your next page list the *financial and abundance wins* you have had. Write why you love to have money. Write about what it can do for you. Do you like to save? Do you have plans for buying a house or a car or going on holiday? Do you have a savings plan? In what way does abundance flow to you, such as friends, holidays, jobs, or nature? How rich is your personal life? Where in the past have you been prosperous and abundant? What have been your successes?

Now write down what the **benefits and rewards** would be of having this area of your life really flow. If you were to step into your power, release, and let go of these reasons of the costs and consequences, how would it improve your life? What would you do? What freedom would that give you? What would that allow you to do now, in one year, and five years from now? What's the importance of this? How committed are you? On a scale of one to 10 (one being the lowest), how committed are you to these improvements?

Commitment: What one action will you commit yourself to and take regarding your financial area, prosperity, and abundance?

Suggested Ideas: Get support and organize a debt payment plan. Open those unopened bills. Understand your money patterns. Make a savings plan. Plan a holiday. Tithe to a charity. Be more grateful for what you do have. Be abundant with yourself.

Day 5: Creativity and Your Inner Child

The expression of your creativity is part of who you are at your core. It is your essence and true reflection of your inner beauty. It is what makes your heart sing and how your passions are ultimately expressed. Your peace and fulfillment come from the expression of who you are. When you are doing something that makes your heart sing, you immerse yourself totally in the activity and lose your sense of time. It is like becoming one with all.

> **Downside:** Unmotivated and feeling dried up
> **Upside:** Play and innocence
> **Keys: Your innate self-expression and curiosity**

How do you feel about your creativity? Read the statements out loud. What makes you squirm? Write down the ones that give you the strongest feeling response and have an emotional charge.

For example:

Have your spark and passion disappeared? Do you feel lost in knowing what you love to do? Have your dreams gone? Were you criticized or humiliated when you were small? Were you made to feel stupid when you were a child? Perhaps you wanted children and the right time or situation never arose? Have you judged yourself for your efforts? Are you frightened to express yourself? Were schooldays enjoyable? Were you bullied at school and picked on by teachers?

> **Tasks:**
>
> After the statements that you have already noted, pick at least three different colored pens (more if you would like). Be creative. Maybe even do your writing on the page differently from, say, a list page; no one is going to see. Draw pictures of how it feels around the statements above. It is for your eyes only! Have fun with this section. Express yourself with your writing about what is going on for you, how you

see your creativity past and present. What are your feelings around this subject? Be expressive! Check in and see how many "I can't" or "I am not good at" statements there are.

Write down the **costs and consequences** to you of not expressing your creativity. What has this meant to you in your life? Where are you stuck? What do you want to change? What are you doing that bores you to tears? What if you do nothing to express yourself because you believe you are not creative? What is the cost of this now? What would be the cost of this a year from now and in five years from now? Thank you for having some fun!

On your next page list any *creative activities* that make your heart sing. What did you enjoy as a creative outlet as a child? What do others do that you are curious about? Is there something you would like to do but you haven't yet? What are your passions? Have you had an urge to learn how to sing or dance? What don't you do that makes your heart sing? How could that contribute to being more expressive?

Now write down what the **benefits and rewards** would be of you expressing your heart's desire. What would it feel like if you lost yourself in something you really enjoyed? How would it be to play with your childlike innocence or play with children more? If you were to step into your creativity, release, and let go of these reasons of the costs and consequences, how would it improve your life? What freedom would that give you? What would that allow you to do now, in one year, and five years from now? What's the importance of this? How committed are you? On a scale of one to 10 (one being the lowest), how committed are you to these improvements?

Commitment: What one action will you commit yourself to and take in exploring your creative expression and curiosity?

Suggested Ideas: Go to an art class. Buy paints and a canvas. Start writing in a daily journal. Go for walks in nature. Study a new subject. Play or learn a musical instrument. Read more often. Spend more time with your children and play. Jump out of plane or go paragliding.

Day 6: Career and Your Life Path

Congratulate yourself! You are on Day 6, over halfway through, and I am sure that some light bulbs are going on, giving you some major insights!

You have been trained since you were knee-high to a grasshopper with the belief that you would have a career—a job! And be employed! The education system has trained you to do one thing and one thing only: to be a follower of the system, to come into line, perform, and be part of the herd. Often you were not given the chance to develop yourself and your innate skills. Today that picture is changing little by little, and gradually the herd mentality is becoming less and less.

Often you end up following a career that was a childhood dream, or you wanted to follow in your parents' footsteps (to get their approval), or went into the family business without any deep thought about what you wanted yourself. You can often feel trapped in a career as an adult because of your lifestyle—the responsibility of partners and children. This all has a high monetary cost. As Robert Kiyosaki says, it is time to get out of the rat race!

Downside: Living an illusion, presenting false masks to the world
Upside: Doing what you love to do passionately
Keys: Your passions and being in the right environment

How do you feel about your career? Read aloud the statements, and see what rings a bell. Write down the ones that give you the strongest feeling response and have an emotional charge.

For example:

Does your health and do your relationships suffer as life seems to be all about work? Are you feeling trapped by your career? Do you feel as though you are on a never-ending treadmill? Is your work environment a constant pressure? Is the world too competitive for you? Are you living your passions? Are you losing perspective of who you are? Are you too tired to enjoy life?

Tasks:

After the statements that you have already noted, sit and write nonstop about how you see yourself and your experiences. List all the areas where you feel defeated. What isn't working for you? What patterns have you created in your work history? Do you create unsympathetic bosses? Do you create competition with work mates? Do you enjoy your work? What are you missing out on in your life because of work? How do you feel about that? Is your life path what you want? What are the unfulfilled dreams that are still in the back closet? Keep that pen flowing until there is no more to write about.

Write down the **costs and consequences** to you personally of what this means to you and how you feel about it. What isn't working any more for you? Where are you not shining your gifts? What don't you enjoy? What do you feel exhausted by? What would you rather be doing with your life? What would you like to change? What is the cost of this now, what will it be a year from now, and what will it be five years from now? Well done for that one!

On your next page list what *skills and talents* you have that make your heart sing. In past situations where have you done well? What skills and talents do you like to express? Where have you been successful in your businesses life? What you are intrigued by? What are your wins? What was your favorite job? What aspect of your job or business do you love the most? What are your most proud moments?

Now write down what the **benefits and rewards** would be of expressing your passions and doing what sets your heart on fire. What would start to shine in you? If you were to step into your power and passions, release, and let go of these reasons of the costs and consequences, how would it improve your life? What freedom would that give you? What would that allow you to do now, in one year, and five years from now? What's the importance of this? How committed are you? On a scale of one to 10 (one being the lowest), how committed are you to these improvements?

Commitment: What one action will you commit to and take regarding exploring your passions, life path, and career options?

Suggested Ideas: Look through magazines for ideas. On paper brainstorm your ideal life path. List all your unfulfilled dreams. Start your own business. (What would it be?)

Day 7: Inner Knowledge and Intuition

Here I am referring to how well you know yourself. This is the most important key of them all! The inscription "Know Thyself" is to be found on a lintel at the Temple of Apollo in Delphi, Greece. It has been used by many a philosopher in the past to explain humankind. If you do not know your inner self well, you can be at the influence of others and external situations, and lose yourself. For your own peace of mind, it is important that this philosophy be adopted and discernment applied.

Honoring yourself at the deepest level of your being is where you start the real process of loving yourself. It is about creating a supportive environment, being respectful to yourself, and putting boundaries in place that support your life. Having daily practice of silence so you can listen to your wisdom, meditation for stillness of the mind, exercising your body, and eating foods that are nourishing, all support you being healthy. This gives you connection to your inner essence, so you can follow your heart's desire and be at one with your inner intelligence!

Downside: Disengaged, numb, empty, and alone
Upside: Connected, trust in self, inner knowing
Keys: Inner knowledge and wisdom

As this is such a key segment, be mindful and especially aware of how you do this process.

How do you feel about your inner knowing? Read aloud the statements and be aware of what really resonates with your inner core being and heart. Write down the ones that give you the strongest feeling response and have an emotional charge.

For example:

Do you value yourself enough to look after yourself? Are you in denial of your true state of being, and what action you could take to change that? Is judgment your constant companion? Does your ego rule you? Do you have regrets about the past? Is forgiveness something foreign to you?

Do you trust your intuition? Are you not doing the spiritual work to get to your core being? Do you numb your pain of emptiness? Have you adopted addictions, habits, or emotional patterns to cover what is inside?

Tasks:

After the statements that you have already noted down, do something first: Take a moment and look—I mean *deeply* look—at yourself in the mirror for 20 seconds or so. How easy is it for you to smile at yourself and say "I love you; I am love" and mean it without squirming?

Now go back to your chair. How well do you currently know yourself? How well do you accept yourself? What questions above hit the nail on the head? Is there more exploration to do? Are you in integrity with yourself? How do you talk to yourself each day? Do you go over past situations and turn them over in your mind time and again? Do you have high expectations of yourself and others? Is *surrender* a word that makes you feel out of your comfort zone? How well do you think you love yourself? How kind are you to you? List all your considerations and how you feel about that.

Write down the **costs and consequences** to you personally of not loving and knowing yourself. What has this done to you in your life? What harm has it caused? What is the truth of what you believe about yourself? Where are you stuck? What do you want to change? What is the cost of this now, and what will it be in one year and five years from now? Keep writing even if you feel uncomfortable. There will be some gems in this for you. Thank yourself for your honesty; I know this is a hard one—probably the hardest, as it really makes you look in the mirror.

On your next page list what you *love* about yourself. Is it your hair, your eyes, your voice, your body, your expression, your smile? This is not time to be shy! What is about your character that sparkles for others to see? Where are you kind and compassionate to others? Do you love how you are with your children? Your friends? What aspects of yourself are you at peace with: your creativity, your joy, your life path? What do others love about you?

Now write down what the **benefits and rewards** would be in your life of being totally your full loving self, recognized for who you are. A state of deep peace was a part of you. You no longer hid your sparkle and expressed your spirit fully for the world to see. If you were to step into your true self and shine, release, and let go of all the reasons of the costs and consequences, how would it improve your life? What freedom would that give you? What would that give you now, in one year, and five years from now? What's the importance of this? How committed are you? On a scale of one to 10 (one being the lowest), how committed are you to these improvements?

Commitment: What one action will you commit to and take in order to get to know yourself?

Suggested Ideas: Meditate daily. Listen to your wise inner voice. Do activities such as yoga or martial arts that will give you an inner sense of peace and serenity. Express yourself creatively. Connect with nature. Garden. Go for a walk on the beach. Start a regular spiritual practice. Write in a journal every day. Get professional support. Be kinder to yourself.

Day 8: Support, Helpful Friends, and Fun

It is vital for you to operate on a well-balanced basis. You have a network of people and contacts around you to support you in your down times, and celebrate and have fun in your up times. You are a member of an inter-dependent species, similar to the cells in your body; they are all unique, each doing their own job, in their own special way. The key here is they are unable to operate without each other. They are independent yet inter-dependent; they operate and communicate as a whole in order for the whole body to work in a synergistic way. You are the same; you need connection with yourself and others to support to thrive.

Downside: Life is boring and dull
Upside: Supportive network and fun
   Keys: Choice, pleasure, and support

How do you feel about this area of your life? Read the statements out loud. What hits the nose on the head? Write down the ones that give you the strongest feeling response and have an emotional charge.

For example:

Have you forgotten what fun is? Are you a loner, and do you feel isolated? Are you shy, and do you find social situations hard? Would you like to have more travel in your life? Are you fearful about traveling on your own? Do you need more friends? Is making friends not easy for you? Have your friends hurt you in the past? Are you too serious and cannot let yourself go? Do you take time to have "time out"? Do you get distracted easily? Is work more important? Do you have too many obligations to others? Do you feel used by your friends?

Tasks:

After the statements that you have already noted, write nonstop about what you know about this area of your life. What areas would you like to improve? What do you miss most in your life around having fun? What are you not doing, like dancing, or going to the movies or the theatre? Maybe it is ice skating, playing a sport, being more artistic, reading, or relaxing. Is it just hanging out with friends? Is it spoiling yourself and getting pampered? Having weekends away or going on holiday? Is there more support you need? Who supports you when you are down? Do you need to build a support network?

Write down the **costs and consequences** to you personally of not having pleasure and fun in your life. What do you miss out on by not having the right friends in your life who support you? What has this meant to you in your life? Are you lonely? Do you keep yourself isolated and separate? What do you want to change? What do you want more or less of? What is the cost of this now, and what will it be a year from now and five years from now?

On your next page list your activities of *fun and hobbies* that you partake in. Where have you traveled that you love? Where else would you like to go? What fond memories do you have of your holidays? Who is in your support network and why are they there? What is it that you like and admire about them? What is good about this area of your life? What do you want more of?

Now write down what the **benefits and rewards** would be of having more fun and pleasure in your life. What would it be like to have more support and a likeminded network of friends? What would it mean to you to travel more, if that is one of your passions? Where would you go? What would you like to see? If you were to open up to others, step into your power, release, and let go of these reasons of the costs and consequences, how would it improve your life? What freedom would that give you? What would this give you now, in one year, and five years from now? What's the importance of this? How committed are you? On a scale of one to 10 (one being the lowest), how committed are you to these improvements?

Commitment: What one action will you commit to and take to having more fun and playtime and getting the right network of support around you?

Suggested Ideas: Blocking time out in your diary for fun time. Join a club of some sort to meet new people. Make plans to go away for a weekend or a longer holiday. Organize fun times with your friends doing out of the ordinary activities. Plan some travel time. Go out and dance.

Day 9: Unity

Here is the final context! When all the above eight areas are in total balance and unity, your life flows, it gets easier, you sparkle, and your life works in amazing ways. You are developing your own oasis—a space of nourishment and enrichment for your soul. This area gives you a reflection of how your life is working.

Downside: Life becomes stagnant and you go against the flow

Upside: You feel integrated and energetic

Keys: Your vibration, balance, flow, and harmony

How do you feel about this area of your life? Read the statements out loud. What hits the nail on the head? Write down the ones that give you the strongest feeling response and have an emotional charge.

For example:

Is life too bleak? Have you forgotten what it feels like for your life to work? Do you struggle being here on this planet? Is life too hard and do you not want to be here anymore? Is it hard for you to surrender to what is? Are you sick of struggling? Is life all too hard?

Tasks:

After the statements that you have already noted, write non-stop about what you know about this area of your life. Has anything become obvious to you that you have not recognized before? What are the areas you would like to improve? What do you miss most in your life?

Write down the **costs and consequences** to you personally of not having unity, balance, and more energy in your life. What do you miss in life? What would make the most difference to you right now? What has this meant to you in your life? What do you want to change? What do you want more or less of? What is the cost of this to you now, in a year, and five years from now?

Write on your next page where you are in *balance and harmony* in your life. What is the one thing that has become glaringly obvious to you about your life through this exercise?

Now write down what the **benefits and rewards** would be if you were able to pull all the contexts together in an integrated whole. If you were able step into your truthful powerful self, and release and let go of these reasons of the costs and consequences, how would it improve your life? What freedom would that give you? What would this give you now, in one year, and five years from now? What's the importance of this? How committed are you? On a scale of one to 10 (one being the lowest), how committed are you to these improvements?

Commitment: What one action will you commit to and so you take your life to another energy level and achieve balance, harmony, flow, and unity in your life?

Suggested Ideas: Commit to a life plan that changes the way you live. Get some professional help to support you in the next step.

Chapter 6

Sorting out Your Story,
and Bringing it All Together

Your fears, beliefs, emotions, decisions, attitudes, mind-
sets, pain, and challenges

"Once you make a decision, the universe conspires to make it happen."

~ Ralph Waldo Emerson

When all the above nine areas are flowing smoothly and you are truly in tune with your song, your energy becomes more highly attuned, balanced, and integrated. This results in unity being experienced and expressed through your essential being with the benefit of the universal flow carrying you through your life effortlessly!

This activity comes in two parts, split into Day 10 and Day 11, and is about pulling all of your inquiry information together. It will give you an overview map or picture of all the information discovered in the tasks that you have done over the past nine days that has created your story to date.

Go with your gut instincts; this is not about getting it perfect. It is a working document that you will use for guidance later.

Day 10: Sorting Out Your Story

Tasks:

Step 1: Go through each category from Day 1 to Day 9 and, with a different colored pen or highlighter, circle the statements and words that jumped out at you.

Step 2: Next, collate information on the three areas in your journal as follows: "What Doesn't Work" (the costs and consequences; this is your Discovery information), "What Does Work" (this is your Awareness information), and "Benefits" (this is your Benefits information).

Step 3: Title your page **"Discovery A-Ha's."** Go through the nine sections and list all those items in the nine different contexts you have circled as being important and that made an impact—the "ouch" items in the Discovery section. When you have finished listing everything, do not judge what you have come up with. It is neither good nor bad; **it just *is!*** You have created your Discovery road map of where you are in your life right now.

Step 4: Title another page **"Awareness Light Bulbs."** Go through the nine sections and list all of those items in the different contexts you have circled relating to your attributes, contributions, wins, skills, talents, passions, and where you shine.

Step 5: Title the next page **"Benefits and Rewards."** Go through the nine sections and list all the benefits and rewards that would flow to you when you change some of your fears, beliefs, and habits, and start jumping off the cliff.

> You now have a good inventory of where you are at this moment of time. Congratulations!

Now it is time for a break. Take some time out, drink water, get a cup of something, go into nature and ground yourself, or put on some loud music and dance around. Thank yourself for the courage you have to go where you may not have gone before. Celebrate what you have just discovered, which is your truth at the moment. Nothing is set in concrete. One thing is for certain: Change is always a constant. Remember: Until you know where you have come from—in particular, where you are now—you cannot know where you want to go!

Well done!

Day 11: Bringing it All Together

Allow yourself as much time as you need. Please do not give yourself time limits, and ensure you will not be disturbed. Have fun with it.

You can do this task, either by writing lists or by brainstorming on large pieces of paper. There are 12 parts to this exercise. Have other writing paper available, as you may want to write down some longer insights that cannot be described by a word on your map. Do whatever feels right for you.

My advice is to make it fun, lighten up the process by using colored pens and paper, and add symbols and drawings. Use as much paper as you need. Put on some soothing music you like (no hard rock at this point, please!) and have a glass of water handy to hydrate your brain.

Discovery A-Ha's Map

Step 1: Loosen up your energy. Put on some dance music, allow yourself to let go and dance for a minute of two, do lots of deep breathing, and enjoy

Step 2: Read through all 10 steps here, so you are clear about the instructions

Step 3: Title three separate pieces of large flipchart paper with these titles:

- "Discovery A-Ha's Map" (map 1).

- "Awareness Light Bulb Map" (map 2).

- "Benefits and Rewards Map" (Map 3).

Step 4: On the Discovery A-Ha's Map, identify the universal fear or fears you have listed that you recognize, and any others that may have popped up. Write them on this map in a way that is creative for you.

Step 5: On the same Discovery A-Ha's Map, check back to the negative emotions you have listed in your journal. Also list any other emotions and fears you have become aware of while doing this exercise. Write down any scenarios that come to mind about how these have affected you in the past in shorthand or with symbols, as well as what defensive behaviors you use when your back is against the wall.

Step 6: Add to your Discovery A-Ha's Map paper any destructive decisions and unhealthy beliefs you have listed in your journal that you have made in past.

Step 7: Add to your Discovery A-Ha's Map any attitudes you have listed in your journal from the Discovery section and any relevant events or relationships.

Step 8: Add to your Discovery A-Ha's Map any mind-set behaviors you have pinpointed in your journal from the Discovery section and any other relevant information.

Step 9: Finally, go back to the Discovery section in your journal, which you have already compiled from the last chapter in the nine different categories. Add to the above items all the costs and consequences you have listed in those nine sections you recognize hamper your movement forward.

Step 10: *Bring it all together. This is a very important step; do not go past it!* Go through all that you have written from all sections and start to mark all the items that have similar themes. These are patterns that run you and have throughout your life. Start seeing the connections and threads that run across the different sections.

These are the keys for you to know that you are not flowing in your truth. Make a list of these; use them as a guide to work with and journal about every day. You can start to explore and understand where your blocks and limitations are, and what is underneath the surface that is not currently apparent. Once you have an awareness of these, you will be in a stronger position to let them go and come from a choice of being.

Take a couple of deep breaths, put your pens down, and take a drink of water. You have completed the Discovery A-Ha's Map.

When you are ready and feel well rested, go to the next section, and complete the Awareness Light Bulbs and Benefits and Rewards Maps!

Awareness Light Bulbs Map

Step 11: Begin your Awareness Light Bulbs Map. Use different colored pens, go back to the Awareness sections of your journal (from Chapter 5), and list your skills and talents, what you are recognized for, your wins, your contributions, and what other people see in you. Be creative with this page. Cut out symbols and pictures that resonate with you and that are a reflection of you. We will come back to this later.

Benefits and Rewards Map

Step 12: Begin your Benefits and Rewards Map. Use the Benefits sections of your journal (from Chapter 5) and write all the benefits to you and what you would gain from starting this journey. Again, be creative with this. Cut out symbols and pictures that related to this. It is your momentum forward. We will come back to this later.

Identifying and Acknowledging What Is

You have done the hard yakka, as we say in Australia. In time you will come to view this as the one of the most important gifts you have given yourself. You now have three maps to take you forward.

The good thing to remember, even though you might not quite believe it, is that the Discovery A-Ha's Map is a story—your story. It is important, as it has gotten you this far in life. *And* it is an illusion; it is not the truth of who you are, the joy at the core of your sparkling essence. Welcome to your new adventure. Discover your true self and the claiming of it back.

Congratulations! You now have the full picture of what really is going on for you. These maps are not set in concrete and will change over time, for the better! There may be other aspects that come to light, both that bother you and maybe some other highlights you have forgotten. That's okay; just add to them. Equally, if something no longer bothers you, cross it off. Remember: no hard criticism or judgment here; it is just your truth at the moment.

I loved, when I did this work for myself, seeing in a few months later how far I had come! When I checked back to my maps, I could cross off items that were no longer an issue and I could feel new, unknown parts of me were shining through. Celebration time had come.

In fact, as each day passes you will find you become lighter and lighter both in your list and in yourself. It gives you a great feeling of relief.

Let it sink in what a wonderful job you done. Thank and congratulate yourself for having the courage to tell your truth and for acknowledging what you have unearthed. Many times we suppress, avoid, resist, and deny this information so it never comes to light.

You have just accomplished a major part of your healing.

At this point, put these three maps away and give yourself a break. Get up, and celebrate in your way. What is your way of celebration? Make sure that you do it in your way. Whatever that is, have fun and *enjoy.*

You will come to learn and understand that being the Master of your life and destiny has many rewards that you would not have dreamed possible. Leading your life this way, you become the conductor of your life!

Section Three

Tools for Your Soul's Journey

Chapter 7

Guidelines from the Universe

Life strategies and principles

"You were born with potential. You were born with goodness and trust. You were born with ideals and dream. You were born with greatness. You were born with wings. You are not meant for crawling, so don't—You have wings, Learn to use them and fly!"

~ Rumi

A conscious choice is to be made to wake up to the reality of your life—about *being* in life, rather than *doing* in life, and consciously aligning and harmonizing with the universe and your true path. The universe gives you opportunities of all sorts that will impact your life so you can learn. Your life is about creating moment by moment. There is nothing else more important.

On your new journey you need support; taking on new strategies on how to operate your life need to be adopted. I call these guidelines. These guidelines can steady you along your path as you grow and give you inner strength as you start to take responsibility for being who you are and for creating the life you want. The guidelines listed below have been the most powerful for me.

By adopting these fundamental guidelines, you are able to start building a strong foundation that is supportive of your growth, stabilizing your feet on the ground as you live on earth, rather than being swept up in the chaos of the times.

As you can see from the past sections and your in-depth inquiry into your life up to now, it can seem as if you have been in the "washing machine of life," and the cycle of going around and around never seems to come to end! You are on a constant cycle, like in the movie *Groundhog Day*: Events and patterns in your life keep repeating themselves over and over with the same results. Even the same types of people keep turning up!

This can get pretty boring, wouldn't you agree? Where have you had this happen?

> *"If you keep on doing what you've always done,*
> *you'll keep on getting what you've always got."*
>
> ### ~ *W.L. Bateman*

Your experience of your family background is a life where you have been trained and brought up with rules, regulations regarding how things are done, how you behave in public, what is appropriate or not, how to speak to others, how you do things (like how to make your bed or even how to do the washing up!). You are trained to adapt to others' ways of doing life!

Some of these patterns you rebel against, and you are very sure that you are not going to follow. However, there are other patterns, limitations, and constrictions that are so ingrained in your cellular memory, that you have no idea they are there. It is only when you become conscious of them you can do something about them or change them.

What I love about this process of discovery and inner work is that— as you slowly start taking more accountability and responsibility for what you are creating in your life, and as you adopt new strategies of not blaming others for your circumstances, being the victim or feeling fearful, and not being accountable or taking responsibility for your life—you start to leave your old patterning and wounds behind. Life seems to get lighter, you become more curious about everything, and your zest for life starts to return.

Below I have listed nine concepts or guidelines that reflect the universal flow and that are there to support you. They build upon each other as an interconnecting web. You may choose these to be a part of your life strategy, as a new foundation for your life. In times of despair, downtimes, or when you are in need, it is very comforting to lean on old wisdoms for support.

Adopting these will give you a way to observe your life from a different perspective, when you gradually start detaching yourself from your mental and emotional patterns of your ego. Your ego is very clever in the way it manipulates you to continue the illusion of who you are not or as described in the Human Design System—the "not self"! The key here is to become the witness of your life and watch yourself live life with a sense of curiosity and wonder.

As cornerstones they provide safety and support. Think of it a bit like being taught the do's and don'ts of how to cross a busy road: Look right, look left, and then look right again. If it's all clear, you may cross! (It may be the other way, depending on where you live, of course!) These guidelines or principles give you foundational guidance of how to operate in your life—an operating system.

Here is an overview of a selection of guidelines, or maybe we should say the *gems of life*!

1. You are inter-connected and one energy field—not separate!

2. You are vibration. Your job is to raise it!

3. Be open to synchronicity. Go with the flow!

4. Change is constant. Embrace it!

5. You create your own reality. What you put out comes back!

6. Your world is your mirror. Be your own guide!

7. What you focus on grows. Energy flows where attention goes!

8. What you resist persists. Accept what is!

9. Obstacles are opportunities. Gifts are given!

1. You Are Inter-Connected and One Energy Field—Not Separate!

"Energy drives everything we do. Energy is the driving force behind our choices, our relationships, our interactions, how we feel and how we move on any given day...."

~ Lee Harris, Ask the Heart (For it Knows Everything)

To understand this concept you need to understand the nature of the universe. Everything is made of energy, but in its form can look different. You are inter-connected and one energy field, not separate beings. It is inspiring to see how science and spiritual teachings are starting to align in their understandings.

Lynne McTaggart says in her book *The Field, "That science has recently begun to prove what ancient myth and religion have always espoused: There may be such a thing as a life-force."* Dr. Wayne W. Dyer says of her work, *"McTaggart presents the hard evidence for what spiritual masters have been telling us for centuries."*

McTaggart also writes: *"What has been discovered is nothing less than astonishing. At our most elemental, we are not a chemical reaction, but are an energetic charge. Human Beings and all living things are a coalescence of energy in a field of energy connected to every other thing in the world. This pulsating energy is the central engine of our being and our consciousness, the alpha and omega of all existence."*

You are not just flesh and bones, physics and biology, as past scientists have believed; you are not isolated or separate beings, pushing your way through life on your own. You are united through an underlying energy field, and all are connected. You can call it The Field, or The Force, as in *Star Wars* (The Force be with you), or The Source.

All of your actions have consequences in the world around you for the very simple reason that you are connected. Similarly, when you throw a stone into a pond, ripples appear on the water's surface, showing it has an effect on its surroundings.

Humans are made up of more than 70 percent water; the planet is 80 percent water. Japanese author Masaru Emoto is experienced in alternative medicine and wrote the book *The Hidden Messages of Water.* Emoto has done many experiments that have been photographed and documented. The amazing results in his book show, quite clearly, that different emotional thoughts, such as love or anger, show up in water that has been frozen into ice crystals. The difference is astounding. So it stands to reason that all your energies are interconnected and have an invisible effect on each other.

In the world today in the name of profit, a lot of damage is perpetrated onto innocent bystanders. If you are all one, why does this happen? It is like you are damaging a part of yourself. Why would you damage something that is part of you—an extension of you?

Benefit: Through this invisible field you are connected to all living things! There is no separation; you are not alone. You are waves of light, connected to the universal energy. You are the microcosm within the macrocosm, a holographic universe in itself. Live your life knowing you are connected to all living things and you are a live network of energy. Ensure that your thoughts, behaviors, and actions support not only you but others around you. Be mindful of the consequences of your actions! Practice having an open, loving heart.

2.   *You Are Vibration. Your Job Is to Raise It!*

"If you send out goodness from yourself,
or if you share that which is happy or good with you,
it will all come back to you multiplied ten thousand times.
In the kingdom of love there is no competition;
there is no possessiveness or control. The more love you give away,
the more love you will have."

~ John O'Donohue, Anam Cara: A Book of Celtic Wisdom

As Maggie Jean Wahls, Shamanic Elder, quotes, *"The single spiral is one of the oldest known symbols in the world. It forms a science called sacred geometry. It has represented the concept of growth, expansion, and cosmic energy. Ancients believed that energy, both physical & spiritual, flowed in a spiral form...."*

Simply put, what Maggie is talking about is that all energy is based on sacred geometry taken from the simple element of the spiral, which observes a distinct mathematical equation: the Fibonacci sequence. This sequence is also found as the basis of the seven tones of music. This simple spiral evolves into more complex shapes upon which the universe is made.

This patterning is in inherent in all things—all nature and human beings alike. Whether you observe a sunflower or ancient symbols or structures such as the Great Pyramid, they all contain this basic design. All of life in the universe is made up of this energy field, based on these mathematical equations and musical elements of vibration and frequency.

As connected human beings living in a third-dimensional world, you are made up of energy in different forms defined as body, mind, and spirit. Your energy has a range of frequency or vibration dependent upon how positive or negative your state of being is at the time.

Your energy spirals up or down, depending upon its vibration or frequency. Your continual expansion will ensure that your energy vibration or frequency increases. That is your job!

Think about the chaos in the world at the moment, the needless wars, the poverty and hunger. Look at the people who are experiencing these situations. How does it make you feel to see the desolation, loss, hopelessness, and despair in these people? Are you feeling happy and positive? Or do you have a heavy feeling in your stomach and heart?

Have you ever entered a room after an argument and everyone is pretending that all is okay, but you get a sense that all is not right, as there is heaviness in the air?

You have some experience with this. Maintaining positive attitudes and emotional states of being keeps your energy field of vibration resonating at a higher level, which in turn magnetizes to you similar vibration levels in the form of events, people, and happenings in your life. It is like an attraction factor.

What is exciting about the understanding and coming together of science and spirit is that your future handling of dis-ease will start to become very different. As you apply the science of vibration by unblocking the energy at its source, the healing of the dis-harmony in the body disappears. As Dr. William Teller states, *"Future medicine will be based on controlling energy frequencies in the body."*

So how you think, feel, and act reflects on how your life unfolds. You have discovered in previous chapters that you have varying thoughts and emotions that have come from your past conditioning. Some patterns and emotions can be hidden from you in your subconscious mind; this often causes conflict and resistances that lower your vibrational state.

The name of the game is to choose activities, attitudes, and thoughts that support, enhance, encourage, and raise your vibration—hence, expand your consciousness field. Consciousness is love, so you are expanding your love frequency. The earth resonates at a particular hertz frequency (528HZ). Out of interest the hertz frequency of unconditional love is the same. The more you connect at that level, the easier it is for the heart to open and heal.

A similar concept, but based on a different mathematical process as the one above, is from David Hawkins, author of *Power vs. Force.* He explains through his Map of the Levels of Consciousness (tested through applied kinesiology practices) the different levels of frequency or energy relating to emotions, states of being, and beliefs.

As Dr. Hawkins points out, the significance lays in the connection between the levels rather than the numbers. These levels have a magnetic pattern connected to them—so if you put out a certain energy frequency, this returns to you in the form of similar energy. Even your state of health vibrates at a certain frequency, as does dis-ease. Yes, dis-ease has a frequency, too!

His map starts from a level of fear-based frequency at 0 to an enlightenment-based frequency of 1,000. From 200 and upward is where you go from the destructive to the positive force energy field. At this frequency you start to see the world differently, waking up to other possibilities rather than experiencing the lower levels of fear and desolation. At 200 you start to become the master of your own destiny.

At the 250 frequency level, trust and safety start to become established, you feel safer in the world, and you are able to begin to surrender and release from your lives what no longer serves you. This is an important level, as you start to see your world with a different pair of eyes and opportunities not previously available start to appear.

He suggests as you rise above this you reach the level of acceptance at 350. This results in the acceptance of yourself as you are. The more you clear out your old patterns and paradigms, your energy frequency increases until you start operating from a higher vibratory level. This in turn allows you to open your hearts and start loving yourself on a more unconditional basis, resulting in more joy, peace and fulfillment.

Benefit: When you become involved with energies that do not match your current state of vibration, you can be dragged down and go into a downward spiral As you become more conscious of your activities, your energy frequency spiral upwards, and new situations and people of similar vibrations appear in your life. So have the intention each day of raising your vibration in an upward direction.

3.   Be Open to Synchronicity. Go with the Flow!

"Be grateful for whoever comes,
because each has been sent as a guide from beyond."

~ Rumi

Synchronicity is like magic. It is the world moving in mysterious ways. It seems to have no sense to its flow, as it doesn't seem to follow an obvious route; it almost seems random, but at the deeper level of things it has purpose. It is the workings of the universe at its ultimate flow. How come, you ask? I understand it as the energy of universal flow doing the work it is here to do: create magic.

As you connect with this energy source, trust it, and become one with it, the universe will send you messages in various guises that you can interpret as a signpost or use as a guide to help direct you where to go next on your path.

Synchronicity is a way of explaining the bringing together of your external world with your internal world of intentions, sometimes in a way that not even you could imagine. Magic!

As Deepak Chopra says: *"My own life has been touched often by synchronicity, so much so that now I get on an airplane expecting the passenger in the next seat to be surprisingly important to me, either just the voice I need to hear to solve a problem or a missing link in a transaction that needs to come together.... I believe that all coincidences are messages from the unmanifest—they are like angels without wings, so to speak, sudden interruptions of life by a deeper level...."*

Have you ever had a problem or challenge that you have been running through your mind that you are unable crack, or you're unable to find the next piece of the puzzle?

You walk down the street and bump into someone you have not seen for ages, the conversation turns to your problem, and you realize you have been given the answer? An e-mail appears in your inbox that has an attachment that gives you your answer?

You may even have been thinking that you would like to connect with a certain person and then the phone rings and it's that person. The universe is working in its mysterious way to support you.

Recently I met a woman at a yoga class. After a short period (an hour), and by having a discussion about glass bottles, we realized she was renting the same house that I had lived in for the previous five months.

What is the likelihood of meeting up with someone in a yoga class, in a place where there are many different yoga studios, in a town full of tourists with a population of approximately 30,000 people? We both lived in different areas of the town, and are both from different parts of the world living here in a foreign country for a few months. What connected us in this random way? Was this coincidence or synchronicity? I think synchronicity.

Since then, a wonderful connection and friendship have been established based upon our similarities. I had the intention of meeting more like-minded people in my life that were on my wavelength. The universe answered my request. I am sure we will be friends and colleagues for many years to come.

Benefit: When you trust and allow the universal flow to support you, magical things happen, and you will be given gifts from source that not even you could have dreamed was possible. Use this energy force well. Be aware and observe, allowing yourself to go with the flow. Get out of your own way and stop trying to control your life. Be open to receiving the gifts that are being sent to you in this random way!

4.   *Change Is Constant. Embrace It!*

"Acceptance is what something seeks to be able to change."

~ *Jennifer Starlight*

In the third dimension, there is one constant thing you can be sure of: Change in your world is inevitable, so don't fight it.

Why is it so hard to accept change and easily make changes? Change makes you uncomfortable, as it takes you out of your comfort zone and what you had planned. You have to let go of control, trust, surrender, and go with the flow.

Change yourself rather than spending hours trying to change others to see your world from your point of view. This is a waste of your energy and an impossible task! Let them be and appreciate them for who they are.

Isaac Asimov said, *"The only constant is change, continuing change, inevitable change that is the dominant factor in society today. No sensible decision can be made any longer without taking into account not only the world as it is, but the world as it will be."*

Your life is made up of lots of little moments of time, and being present in those bits of time requires you not to be casting back to your constructed past memories, or checking out the horizon with your concerns.

In fact, in each and every moment there is a *new* moment that you experience. To live life fully you need to get your head around the concept that there is no time, per se. There is no past and no future; it is all a consequence of perception that creates this illusion of separation of time. In other words, there is only now and you only have this moment that you are living. Be with and live your experiences as though they are new to you.

Watch how a baby or a child is mesmerized by life in the moment. He or she is so absorbed into whatever he or she is doing that immersion is total. Where is the past or the future for this child? He or she is totally absorbed in the present.

I love the word *present*. It is a gift—a present and pre-sent! This is how a child is in the present, as though he or she has been given a gift.

Change affects every area of your life: your career, your health, and your finances. Change happens in your family life and relationships, in your friendships, and in the world at large. You cannot fight this. Ask yourself this question: What are the things I can do to harness this constancy of change for my own good and that help me in life? *Find ways to embrace change.* Come from your true essence, a place that has constancy and gives you the strength to flow with external changes.

For me, welcoming change has been my hardest challenge. After recently arriving to live in a third-world country, my first few weeks were a total nightmare. I was presented with change almost constantly. I remember the anxiety that I created for myself in just trying to hold onto some semblance of order through the chaos! I soon got the message.

There are five parts to the learning I had—with benefits:

1. Have no expectations or assumptions about plans. The universe has other ideas.

2. Have no attachments to outcomes. The outcome is usually better than the plan.

3. Totally surrender to what is. Enjoy the benefits of surprise happenings.

4. Be open to the flow of the universe. It is far less stressful.

5. Be grateful for everything given. Open the heart to joy and peace.

So, you see, the major benefit was learning to surrender, trust, and let go of any perceived vision of how I thought it should be—and have no attachment to a specific outcome. Once I was in that space of coming from a true sense of my inner being, I was always supported by the universe, whatever happened.

Use change as a tool; it helps change your reality. If there is something that you are not happy about in your life, change it! Change can be considered hard if your old beliefs, fears, attitudes, and behaviors are set in concrete. There is no getting away from it; change is related to your growth as a human being. If you stay the same you become stagnant in whom you are, inflexible in your ways, and usually not much fun!

The universe gives us the gift of change. Use it as a tool and an opportunity for expanded awareness. The biggest gift for you is the one of connection to *your inner knowing*. So listen inside, and be quiet enough to hear the messages that come through.

Benefit: The game with change is trying to manage the trends inherent in change. How do you manage change? Study change and you will find out. Change is a far easier thing to manage than you may imagine. Changing is choosing to go with the flow—doing things differently from what you normally do. It is nothing more, and nothing less.

Take gentle action in the direction of change, one step at a time. It is like the acorn; you plant it, nurture it, and water it, and in its own time will grow into a magical oak tree. Just like you!

---

6.   *You Create Your Own Reality. What You Put out Comes Back!*

"Life is an echo: what you send out comes back."

~ Chinese proverb

I come from Sydney, Australia, where an object used by the Aboriginal races for many centuries is a boomerang, a throwing stick that comes back.

This is a great analogy to explain creating your own reality: What you put out to the universal energy field comes back! It does not matter what it is; the energies will match up. If you send out love, kindness, or gentleness, *or* anger, sadness, fear, or contempt, it matters not; it will come back to you as a reflection in leaps and bounds.

So how do you create your reality?

Through the *choices* you make. The thoughts you think. The emotions you feel. The attitudes you hold. The decisions you make. The beliefs you hold and the values you base your actions upon.

Obviously some of these are not always coming from the conscious mind. Remember that some of these beliefs and decisions get stored in the subconscious mind, from the patterns of your childhood. You often carry these in your persona and your energy fields like a flag or badge, announcing to the world this is who you are and what you think of yourself. The universe very kindly sends this energy back to you as reflections, thinking this is what you have asked for.

The late Jane Roberts, author of *The Nature of Personal Reality,* spoke for Seth in her material:

> *"Your beliefs form reality. Your individual beliefs and your joint beliefs. Now the intensity of a belief is extremely important....*
> *And, if you believe, in very simple terms, that people mean you well, and will treat you kindly, they will. And, if you believe that the*

world is against you, then so it will be in your experience. And, if you believe...if you believe that you will begin to deteriorate at 22, then so you shall.

And, if you believe that you are poor, and always will be, then so your experience will so prove to you. Your beliefs meet you in the face when you look in the mirror. They form your image. You cannot escape your beliefs. They are, however, the method by which you create your experience."

I liken it to ordering a dish at a restaurant. You order a healthy dish to eat, such as grilled fish and salad, but in your deepest being you desire a big bowl of pasta with a rich cream sauce, followed by sticky date pudding and ice cream!

Well, what happens? The universe is like a restaurant kitchen; you order one thing consciously and subconsciously wish for another. The universe gets confused. It sends your deepest desire—your subconscious wish. The reason for this? Your subconscious wish has a stronger vibration than what you are consciously thinking about. It is the nature of the game! If you can get your sense of humor into perspective, it can be very funny!

How many times have you complained that it doesn't matter what you do—you experience what you don't want? Situations and people turn up in your life showing you what you are really sending out.

You need to pay attention to your thoughts and actions, even the little ones of not being present, or being in another time or place. Maybe you are in a state of worry about something and feel grumpy and having a bad hair day; without thinking, you brush people off with unkindness or rudeness.

You may be surprised at being given a gentle prod as the same energy comes back to you. At this time you are not totally present, it is comes to you as a surprise and often you didn't see it coming. It is like that boomerang: It does come back!

Benefit: Everything is mirrored back to you by the universe. Allow yourself to understand the boomerang messages and use them wisely to your own advantage. Allow them to guide you, and be a witness and observer to what is going on in your life. This way, you will start uncovering some of the hidden gems giving you the keys to your life.

7.   *Your World Is Your Mirror. Be Your Own Guide!*

*"Seek what is behind the reflection in the mirror,
for there you shall find your bliss."*

~ Jennifer Starlight

Your outside world is a reflection of yourself in some way. How cool is that?

This mirror is there for you to be able to see your total reflection, so you can identify how your life is going and which direction you are heading. Think of it as a general report card on the circumstances of your life.

I call these reflections signposts; they are directions on what to do and where to go next. Call it the bridge to self-knowing. The key is how to read this map. It is in a different language than what you are used to. It is like a cipher code: Until you have the code you cannot read what is being sent to you. This is a powerful way for you to be accountable for your actions and take responsibility. I like to see responsibility not in a heavy light, but how are you responding to the situation (respond-ability).

"... Your internal state is easier to control than what you perceive around you. It is much easier to eliminate hatred from within you than from the rest of the world. However trying to rid the entire world of hatred can seem considerably harder, and impossible. The key to banishing something from your external world, is to eliminate it from your internal world..."

~ From MindReality.com

How do these signposts show the way? How can you get them to work for you?

An external event or circumstance happens that creates an emotional response in you. For instance, you may feel angry, sad, or confused. Your internal response will be to protect or defend yourself around this. To avoid feeling more pain, you project that pain onto another, especially in the form of anger! (Nice one, eh?)

This is based on old patterns you have developed over time, protecting you from feeling pain and keeping you safe. When you have another similar experience, old feelings that have not been resolved from automatically get triggered. Responses are stored in the subconscious. This is a great method for you to see what is stored inside you.

When you project your fears and insecurities outside of yourself onto others, your interpretation of what gets reflected back to you are filtered through your own wounded lens of perception. Often this triggers those unresolved deep wounds you carry. As you can see, these reflections give you an understanding of what is going on at the deepest level. It is like seeing your projection on a movie screen. You are the audience, seeing your life being played out before you, either as a drama or soap opera!

Very often you may not understand how the trigger came to be until you gently delve a little deeper. This is time for you to get to work and discover what it is from your past that has been spotlighted. With a little practice of mindfulness you will become very proficient.

The good news is that once you have the "a-ha" about what is going on and understand the reflection and own it as yours, the pattern and reflection disappear and the emotional charge ceases.

Benefit: This allows you to release the old baggage from your life. When a signal or a warning bell rings and you are alerted to the fact that an outside event has caused an upset, review the feeling it has brought by inquiring how it relates to what you projected outside of yourself. What is the first thing that comes to mind? Trust this response. This guideline is one that can serve you well, so choose what you want in your life each day and be mindful!

8.   *What You Focus on Grows. Energy Flows Where Attention Goes!*

"The cave you fear to enter holds the treasure you seek."

– Joseph Campbell

What you focus on grows. Your energy is immediately magnetized where you put your focus. If it is positive this is what will grow; if it is negative that is what will grow. It is like the analogy of seeing the glass half full or empty.

The enormous energy it takes to hold negative energy in place often results in exhaustion and burnout. By holding this energy deep down and often ignoring it, you are in truth focusing on what doesn't work as you are avoiding it! Know that where your attention/energy goes, it always grows. So be aware of where you are putting your attention!

One of the tools of neuro-linguistic programming (NLP) is a method that highlights whether you are coming from a motivation based in the past that you are running away from (for example, are you motivated by something you don't want, like being overweight, so you create overweight?), or are you motivated by something that you want to go toward in the future, avoiding the past, like an expectation of a different life?

Coming from the past or going toward the future only increases your anxiety, fear, and stress levels. Consequently you are not in acceptance of what is in happening in the present moment, including any feelings or emotions.

The first key here is acceptance and acknowledgment of what is, and the second is surrendering to that. Acceptance is a powerful tool on your growth and expansion journey. There is no resistance in acceptance. When we accept, we acknowledge the status quo, the facts of what is. It is neither good nor bad; it just is! So when looking at what doesn't work in your life, your financial situations, your relationships etc., see the honest truth. Don't judge yourself. Don't let your inner critic go on a rampage. See it from the perspective of "so it is."

What is surrender? Surrender is letting go, not in the sense that you surrender to the other side as in war, or resign yourself to something you don't want; it is about surrendering to the situation as it is, allowing the universal energy to support you in its magical ways, and trusting in that flow.

The book *Jonathan Livingston Seagull,* written by Richard Bach, tells the wonderful story of a seagull's life journey and how he learns to have the courage of his own convictions to live his own life to the full and follow his passions.

Which area of your life do you need to reclaim and let fly? Is it in your relationships, your career, your life direction, your creativity, or another area of your life?

My experience with this area was making the decision to go overseas and take a break from my life. Metaphorically speaking, I jumped off the cliff and flew. I packed all my belongings and put them in storage, gave my notice on my apartment, and took a new adventure.

I knew it was the right thing to do, as everything in my life had become stagnant. I needed to make a change and take another path. I needed to let myself free, and stop repeating patterns of the past, stop avoiding my fears of the future, and start experiencing a more rewarding and meaningful life.

Jumping off the cliff allows you to be caught and supported by the wind, so you can live from your heart and make your own rules and be ultimately free.

Benefit: Wherever you put your attention, this grows. Have the intention of what you would like to experience each day; wake each morning and put out your intention in a positive way. Come from a space of strong intention or resolve of how your day will be, such as joyful and adventurous (not

"I don't want to experience this or that"). If some other ugly thoughts appear—and they may—just notice them in passing and get back to your intention! This is the power of witnessing at work for you!

9.   *What You Resist Persists. Accept What Is!*

"It is an honour to see a soul surrender to the God of their being. So dear ones rest, surrender and receive."

~ Min via Jennifer Starlight

Carl Jung said, *"What you resist persists."* This is a natural law of the universe. It is about accepting and not avoiding what is present in the moment. When you resist what is, you are empowering and magnifying what is there and attract more of the same. Where your attention goes, your energy goes—and creates, whether you want it or not!

As already discussed, change is the norm. Accept change and do not resist! Otherwise more pain transpires. You end up hitting your head against a brick wall that you cannot break through.

I love this thought from Eckhart Tolle: *"When we've suffered enough we'll be ready to surrender, to let go and to stop resisting what is."*

The important words here are *suffered, resisting,* and *surrender.*

Resistance is useful only to the degree that it helps you grow; to continually use it as a defense mechanism to keep you safe is insane! Often you argue for your limitations, which gives you enormous suffering, as you want everything to be just right and you do not want to relinquish control to the unknown.

The resistance you put in place is to avoid feeling old pains and memories from the past, buried deep within your psyche. I call this self-punishment. Somehow it is easier to avoid the old pain than letting go and surrendering to what is and could be. Why do you resist so much? Why punish yourself? The ego wants to avoid feeling more of the old pain, avoiding at all costs experiencing surrender and letting go. Does this seem like a paradox?

You label and judge your childhood painful experiences as good or bad, and lock them into your subconscious. These are there as a constant reminder that to experience those pains again is all too painful. You avoid it at all costs, until the pain is too great.

You strengthen what you oppose, keeping the status quo of being separate from all there is. As you label or judge things you create an emotional attachment around them, rather than just seeing them as they are.

You may have thoughts like "I don't want to create more debt" and "I never want another relationship like that one again." These thoughts are creating resistance, and what you resist persists. This pain is asking for you to pay attention so you can get your life back into harmony; denying it or avoiding it only creates more struggle and pain.

My personal experience in this area was about my financial inheritance. I was so determined to make it grow. I studied and studied how to invest correctly. I thought the investments I chose were safe; I watched them closely for six months. Unbeknown to me, hidden deep below was the fear that I didn't want to fail. The end story was I lost it all, through the fear I put out, which had a greater energy impact than my belief in my abilities.

So the questions I have for you are: How much do you want to suffer? How much do you need to suffer? How much pain do you want? How much punishment do you want? Do you know when you have had enough suffering? When is enough, enough? When are prepared to drop your resistance and look at what needs to be embraced?

Benefit: By letting down your defenses, accepting, and not resisting, you go past the emotional attachment and allow yourself to feel underneath. You are then able to release this pent-up energy and redirect to other areas of your life, reclaiming that part of your essential nature. When we offer no resistance to what is and not label it, the emotional charge disappears.

10. *Obstacles Are Opportunities. Gifts Are Given!*

"Nothing is impossible, the word itself says, I'm Possible."

~ Audrey Hepburn

In every obstacle or challenge you face, know there is a tremendous opportunity, and a gift is given—hidden deep within, like a pearl of wisdom or a blessing in disguise—that serves you on your life's journey. When you get the gift, it sparkles for you like the light and diamond you are, and you become the gift you are!

You come to your wisdom through the learnings you experience through life. They are what give you inner strength and give you wisdom. These gifts are sent for the purpose of overcoming adversity, and learning about aspects of yourself and your soul. This allows you to grow and stand tall. So welcome them in with open arms.

Beyond the pain and hurt of a broken relationship, grief in the death of a loved one, or regret over decisions made regarding your personal finances, lies a lesson for you to learn about yourself. Maybe the learning is to love yourself unconditionally, coming from a place of inner strength, learning to be your own person, letting go of judgments of yourself, and truly valuing yourself for who you are, not what you have. Whatever it is, it teaches you that you are a miraculous being of divine energy and are perfect in that.

As a child you were led to believe that you made mistakes. You were taught that you had to get it right. You take this with you into adulthood and become paralyzed by fear of getting it wrong.

Let's get a new perspective. There are no mistakes, only learning.

The process of learning is to practice, and when practicing something new, you have to keep doing it until you feel confident enough that you have learned the new skill. This is how you get it the way you want it. It is like learning how to ski or ride a bike; you get on, you fall down, you do this a few times, and you get the hang of it. Life is the same. You make mistakes many times until you learn the skill.

Don't take things so personally. If someone is projecting his or her stuff at you, check in with yourself: If this is your stuff (if so, then own it), or is it his or hers? Why is it presenting itself right now? This is the time to learn about detachment and understand how well you have established your own personal boundaries of what is okay for you or not.

When you argue or fight with the boulders that get put on your path, you give away your energy to this thing and become attached to it, losing the perspective of the higher vision of you.

I know sometimes you just like to wallow in the drama of it all! Allow yourself a little time to do this, and then get pen and paper and answer some questions. Ask yourself: *Is this my stuff or someone else's? What am I not seeing clearly? What is my learning? What is the lesson? What emotions does it bring up for me, what do I feel (such as fear, anger, or loss)? What are the steps I can take to let it go? What are the actions I can take?*

See these obstacles with curiosity; play with them. What are they trying to tell you? Don't let avoidance or distraction of other things in the door, confront the obstacles head-on. Take a deep breath and see it for what it is.

A clue here for when issues come up and push your buttons: Check whether there is more than one issue being presented at this time. If there is, it can muddy the water and often makes the problem(s) seem bigger, and this can become overwhelming. When you check in and inquire with yourself this way, clarity has the space to bubble up, and suddenly everything becomes more manageable.

Recently I had to make a decision about renting a new house. It was hard to make a clear decision and it felt complicated. I was certainly making it much more difficult than it was. I enlisted the help of a friend to listen to my challenge, and with her help I understood there were two issues relating to the decision. One was the cost of the house; the second was that I would need some sort of personal transport, like a car or motorcycle, to get into town, as the house was so far out. Once that was understood, my decision became clear in an instant, as I had the full picture of what was really going on!

Benefit: Obstacles are gifts given. Holding onto situations that hurt only destroy you in the end, resulting in more stress, bad health, and a life that does not work or support you. Three keys can assist you in flowing with this guideline:

1. Being in a state of self-forgiveness, and understanding that you are creating these obstacles to learn and grow.

2. Accepting what is and being grateful for what you are given.

3. Knowing that there no mistakes, only learning!

***

Have a gratitude diary that you write in each day. Note even the smallest things you are grateful for, and you will experience your life differently. Being grateful on a daily basis certainly enhances your energy field.

All of these guidelines can support you strongly in your life, and act as a foundation tool for you to grow strong and accountable for your life. Adopt and use them; you will experience life differently!

Chapter 8

Personal Values

Your inner guidance system

"There is no other greater ecstasy, than to know who you are."

~ Osho

I want to turn your attention to your personal values, or principles, and the importance that these have in your life, as they interlink with the guidelines.

Knowing your personal values is one of your most precious assets, and they do change throughout the different stages of your life. By being aware and living by your own set of values, you are given focus and clarity; it is like having your own personal antenna—a compass of your inner knowing and intuition. Your values are your inner guidance system.

Your internal guidance system gives you insight into who you are and what is important at the deepest level so you can live in harmony with your essential nature. Every individual has a different set of these core principles.

It is important your values do not conflict, as they drive your behavior and consequently your flow. The key is not to deny and turn away from this part of you and allow yourself to get distracted by seemingly more important things.

We are now going to identify your values.

Note: When doing this exercise, be especially conscious of the fact they are not driven by your egoic or personality nature, but rather come from the space of your inner intelligence.

Eliciting and Prioritizing Your Values

For the purpose of this exercise, concentrate on your overall values. These values can interlink across different areas, such as physical, interpersonal, psychological, family life, and career.

You may relate to some of these values: freedom, peace, life direction, love, trust, truth, learning, security, intimacy, adventure, well-being, compassion, kindness, respect, beauty, contribution, self-expression, courage, simplicity, fairness, honesty, caring, loyalty, vitality, curiosity, spiritual life, travel, children, and family. (And there are more!)

Brainstorm your own list. Be creative about it, using colored pens, and make yourself comfortable. Play some soothing music, or even sit in nature and give yourself uninterrupted time to do this.

Step 1:   **Brainstorm.** Take a deep breath and sink down to your gut. Be still and wait for the answers. Do not do this exercise from your head. Ask yourself the following question: *Truthfully what are the most important things to me in my life?* Keep writing down all the ideas that come to you. If you get stumped, repeat the question. Go for about three or four minutes or a little longer; don't stop until you have asked yourself the question at least three times.

Step 2:   **Identify your top seven.** Go through your brainstorming list and pick out the seven values that jump out and resonate. Write these down on a new piece of paper.

Step 3:   **Prioritize.** Pick the value at the top of your list and ask if it is more important than the next one on your list. If the second one is more important, move it to the top of the list. Do this with each of the values you have on your second list, each time asking: *What is more important to me?*

This will establish the order of your top seven values. Number them from one to seven, with number one being the most important to you; this gives you a baseline to work with.

Step 4:   **Re-evaluate.** Return to your brainstorming list. Check each value against the *seventh* value on the top-seven list. Ask the same question when checking each: *Is this value more important to me than the last one of my list?* Feel for the answer deep inside; if it is not more important, go onto the next value.

Continue through your entire brainstorming list. If any of your values are more important than the last one on your top-seven list, for the moment make a note of them and continue with checking through your list until it is finished.

Step 5:   **Re-check.** Return to the values that you noted as being more important than your number-seven value. Repeat Step 4, asking: *Is this value more important to me than the last one on my list?*

You now have a comprehensive list of your top seven values in your life; this is your inner guidance or compass system. Check over your list; you may be surprised at some of the inclusions!

Well done!

Reviewing Your List

As your list is a picture of where you are currently headed, the next piece is to examine them against any future vision or important dreams you may have to identify any unnecessary conflicts between the values.

For instance, if you have family or relationship at the top of your list and suddenly you were offered your dream job that took you away from your family or relationship, what would you do? Is there a conflict for you? Is there a change you need to make in your priorities?

You may have trust and fairness as important to you, and you work for a company that does not operate from that space, both in the ethics of the company and/or the management of the company. Maybe the management of the company is okay and you have a conflict with your immediate boss. This can generate conflict with your inner values and be disconcerting, and makes it difficult for you to perform to your excellence. If you are in a space for eight to 10 hours a day that is not supportive, over time you can become worn down and start to question your abilities, and your health can suffer. You can ask the question "Is it worth it?"

This is a way to establish more clarity about your values and direction. These are not set in stone. Your top value may not change throughout your life; however, sometimes the ones down the list can change, dependent upon the stage of life you are in.

You can probably see how your values can change when your life circumstances change. For instance, when you are in your 20s, having more adventure may be important to you, whereas when you get into your 30s you might be keener to develop your career and family areas. By the time you get to you 50s and 60s your interests in life may have changed again.

The other thing to point out here is that sometimes when you start to unravel more of your story and the patterning you have adopted (not your true self), you may have a lightning flash that you have adopted some of your family's values and not your own (for example, you think that having a secure job and supporting your family financially is more important than expressing your passions in another career; or you think that you should be a wife and a mother, and not express your creativity in a pursuit that would give you a business and make you a working mother).

Task: Add your top seven values to your Awareness Light Bulb Map, along with a small précis of what this means to you. Cut out and add pictures that relate to each value on a feeling basis. These values are like your rudder, with which you use to steer your life in the direction that honors your true self.

My suggestion is that you review your list every six to 12 months. To review, do the following:

Step 1:   Take a few minutes to sit and write about each value. What do these values mean to you now? What opportunities can you see by having these values? Do they affect any of your dreams? Are they in line with your dreams? Are there any conflicts that come to mind?

Step 2:   Review this writing against your life direction and where you are now headed. Do any of your values need to change position of importance? If so, change the order of their listing now. By doing this, you will recognize how in tune with yourself you are.

Once you have a handle on how to do this exercise, at your leisure go into a little more depth and explore this exercise using the major contexts of your life: relationships, career, spiritual, family. Often they are the same, but sometimes you can get a surprise. If this is the case, you need to be conscious of any potential conflicts that may arise.

When you are living from this aligned space, you will be in flow with the universal energy and be supported on your life journey. When things go haywire in your life, check in with your values. There is a message being given! Change direction; re-evaluate.

This is a great way for you to achieve much more clarity in your life, allowing alignment and harmony to flow through your life.

Chapter 9

The Magic Bullet

Forgiveness and compassion for self

"Be naked in the splendor of the truth of who you are."

~ Gangaji

Over the years of my life, struggles I have encountered have been somewhat accompanied and overwhelmed with a busy mind. The words *ought* and *should* have been strongly used. I have learned this is not helpful mind chatter! It gives the ego full reign over my soul's journey, wanting full control over my life. I am in the way of my own journey. This leaves no room for the universal flow to support and assist in growing and learning about my true self.

This was irrelevant to whatever challenging situation I was experiencing. It could have been a relationship that didn't work out. My finances had become unmanageable. What to choose relating to a career path, or how to handle difficult family communications. When seeking the answers with a judgmental attitude, being in denial, feeling guilty, making assumptions, or having unrealistic expectations of me or others just did not work.

I realized there had to be another link. My understanding was this: I came to comprehend that it starts with the overview that as you journey along your path, you first need to understand which pathway you are traveling! There are two: One is the ego; the other is the spirit.

You have a choice of going the way of the ego, fighting your way up the mountainside through the sticks and stones of life, creating illusion. Or you can choose to go up the side of mountain that is the way of trust and faith, being supported no matter what by your higher self and universal energies. One pathway leads you up the separation highway and doing it all yourself; the other pathway leads you up the oneness highway and receiving universal support.

Which path are you traveling along?

If you are all one and energetically interconnected, then everything outside of you is an illusion you have created through your projected perception. Remember: Everything that comes to you from outside of you is only a reflection what is inside of you, through your projection and perception of that projection. Your thoughts determine your experiences of life, not what happens in your life!

All the struggles, the pain, the challenges, and the ways the ego creates to continually try and seek its way to wholeness—is the wrong path. The way back to your divinity is through your internal process and is the way to undo the ego's control.

I knew to live in a more peaceful and loving way, there must be another key that I could turn to making my life easier.

Well, the key was simple and yet hard to apply. It is in the simplicity of adopting the attitude of true forgiveness and compassion for self from a spiritual basis, not ego basis. Yes, it starts with you!

Earlier in the book I shared universal guidelines for supporting you along this journey, and one of them is that there is really nothing outside of yourself. It is all a reflection; there is only you. Taking accountability and responsibility for everything outside of yourself and applying this one key as mind-set behavior in your life, makes you come from a strong platform as you journey along.

Undo the ego by making your soul journey your primary focus. Listen to your intuition. Surrender to what is, and apply a forgiveness and compassionate mind-set to your journey and allow your gratitude to flow. Allow yourself to be supported. It is a softer path to travel, and inner peace finds you more easily.

Forgiveness becomes your ally—an automatic tool. Everything that is outside of yourself you have created for the purpose of coming home to yourself, to that deep inner part of you. As you let go of the hold of the ego, you will start to recognize your own truth and sovereignty shining through. So everything and everyone who pushes your buttons, forgive. All aspects of yourself that don't sit right with you, forgive. Allow the universal spirit to support you in your forgiveness.

Your natural birthright is one of freedom from limitations, pain, fear, and struggle—to know yourself as the human spirit that you are. For this to come to you, you need compassion for yourself, love for yourself, and acceptance. To know the inner you means there are no barriers or walls, and you come from a place of there is nothing to lose.

In the end you are forgiving yourself for your separation from your source.

Forgive yourself for your beliefs, attitudes, emotions, behaviors, and judgments; they are not who you are at your deepest core. Forgive yourself for the guilt of separation—of taking yourself along the path away from your deepest core. Indeed, honor, and respect that place deep inside. Give yourself permission and the freedom to be all that you are!

I have found this to be a very important link and a more direct route to undoing your ego and traveling toward your essence—your true self. When I started applying this mind-set, my life (and, funnily enough, the people around me) changed quickly, miracles happened, and my life became a life of flow. So start today!

For more information on the "how to" of forgiveness, go to Chapter 10, and read the forgiveness section in "Long-Term Activities: Tools for the Authentic Path"!

You can never lose the truth of whom and what you are; you can only deny it. So as you start to allow and accept what is, forgive yourself, and become aware of the deep stillness within, your life becomes a reflection of what is inside. Receive yourself in your glory.

Chapter 10

How to Support and Heal Yourself along the Way

Tips to assist you on your journey

"I am not what happened to me, I am what I choose to become."

~ *Carl Gustav Jung*

I am taking as a given that you have committed yourself to this journey and are looking forward to taking the steps along the road. *Trepidation* may be a word to explain how you feel, or maybe it is *curiosity* and *excitement?*

Let's get started with the activities that you can use as personal support. They will further establish the commitment that you have made to yourself in taking this journey, and create discipline and guidance along the way. Be regular with your activities; it tells your universe you are serious! It is a way in which to support your spiritual practices and makes them more concrete.

I will give you both daily habits and long-term actions you can use to explore, balance, and stabilize your life.

131

Daily Rituals

These activities are to be done on a daily basis. The process doesn't take long, but it does give you a sense of purpose and direction for the day and supports your spiritual practice. There are seven steps in the morning and seven in the evening; both take approximately 10 minutes. I was given some of these by a spiritual teacher and found them very grounding.

In the Morning

1. Don't get out of bed until you are happy. If you are not feeling that way, change your state by envisioning something that puts a smile on your face. Do a good cat stretch, give yourself a good hug, surround your body with white light, and take it into the body. You can then seal it if you would like with another color.

2. Surrender any expectations you have of the day or attachments to people you may have, and ensure you have a forgiveness and compassionate mind-set in place.

3. Jump out of bed, stretch, dance, do a yoga practice, or tai chi, get your body moving for at least five minutes. If you would prefer you could take a short walk, ground yourself by putting your feet barefoot on the ground, take in nature's energy, or hug a tree.

4. Squeeze the juice of a half a lemon, with added ginger if it suits your taste, and mix with hot water. This helps cleanse and alkalize the body. If you're in the tropics, drink young coconut water.

5. Write some morning pages in your journal; it helps empty the mind.

6. If you choose, pick a guidance card for the day and reflect what that means to you. Maybe note this in your journal.

7. Make a daily commitment to your journey, being ever mindful and aware, and remind yourself to see your day in presence and as an observer with no attachments.

In the Evening

1. Eat at a sensible hour so digestion can complete (at least three hours before retiring).

2. Stop watching TV or working at your computer at least an hour before going to bed.

3. Ensure your bedroom is conducive to sleep. Light sleepers may need a totally darkened room to give you the correct rest.

4. If you have a small problem bothering you, write for five to 10 minutes to get it off your mind. Write up to five things you were grateful for during your day

5. Do not go to bed if there is something not complete with you partner.

6. When in bed, clear your mind of your day. Take a quick whizz through your day by going backward and revisiting your activities. When you have done this, see your mind as a waterfall washing everything away so you rest easily.

7. You may choose to go to sleep with relaxing music playing gently in the background.

Long-Term Activities: Tools for the Authentic Path

In this section I give you more general actions that cover all areas of your life. Treat these like a menu of tips or tools; ask yourself what is going to satisfy the hunger of your spirit when you are choosing for yourself. I call them "tools of the authentic path."

Or, if you want to be more specific, choose the tools that support a category used in Chapter 5, such as relationships or career; whatever speaks to you is okay.

If you experience some mental friends along the way trying to distract and take you away from these exercises, call them imps, gremlins, goblins, bogeymen, elves, or leprechauns, or even give a name them. Their whispering comments could sound like "You don't need to do this," "You haven't got time and you have more important things to do," "I'm too tired," "I don't want this anyway," "It will be too painful," or "It's a waste of time." This is just your ego doing its mind chatter. Thank it for sharing and let it go. You will find your own way to handle them over time!

Breathe

If you are not an exercise fanatic, ensure that you get into the habit of doing deep breathing that reaches down into your navel area. Breathing helps you take in new oxygen and breathe out old, stagnant energy and toxins. Breathe consciously for at least five minutes a day.

Water and Liquids

Keep hydrated all day. You easily get dehydrated when you are in air conditioning, using the computer all day, doing heavy manual work, or physically exerting yourself through exercise. When under stress, the body needs more water, and you can get depleted easily in today's environment, particularly the brain.

Consume at least eight glasses of filtered water a day. (Tap water contains different chemicals and sometimes chlorine and sometimes fluoride.) Note that I said water, not coffee or fruit cordials; these are not water! If you're exceptionally thirsty, add a small amount of apple juice to your water; it is a natural hydrator.

Diet

Eat a balanced diet, with lots of fresh vegetables, and go easy on the fruit, as it is a sugar (albeit a natural one). Be aware of balancing your carbohydrate and protein intake. Eat organic foods where possible to avoid further contamination of pesticides. Ensure that you eat good fats.

Avoid sugar and GMO (genetically modified organisms) foods; you do not have the enzyme capacity to break down these foods. Some of our meat and fish products are farmed with hormones in the animals' food; this gets carried through to the end product that we eat. The increase in dis-eases in the population (for example, diabetes, obesity, and high blood pressure) has been correlated with this fact.

In my experience it is better to start your day with some kind of protein and by eating a good, solid breakfast; it will set you up for the day. Not feeling hungry in the morning is an indicator of your digestion not working efficiently. Take a course of digestive enzymes and probiotics, get the digestion woken up! You need both.

Eat and chew your food slowly. This enhances enzymes in your mouth to assist digestion.

Eating late at night is not good for your digestion. Your body requires at least three hours to digest food properly, so don't go to be bed on a full stomach. For people wanting to lose a little excess weight, consume all carbohydrates by lunchtime, not in the evening. Be mindful of your blood type, as you may be eating foods that your digestion cannot tolerate, such as gluten, grains, and dairy.

Clearing and Cleansing Heavy Metal and Chemical Toxins from the Body

Toxins come in various forms, and all need to be cleared out of the body, whether they originate from emotional stress, environmentally, or from household products.

The environment you live in is heavily contaminated with different heavy metals, which you take into your system and which damage your cells. Make a habit of doing mini body cleanses or fasts to clear out the toxins in your body. Take the pressure off the liver, kidneys, and blood, and allow your body to take a rest. Be gentle with these cleanses. Start with a day at a time and then, if you feel okay, increase to a possible three- to five-day cleanse. Stop if you do not feel okay. Research well. Be careful when doing cleanses, as you need to rest when doing them, and not be busy and stressed. You will be rewarded with increased energy and vitality, and go back to eating slowly.

Drinking warm water, rather than cold, helps to clear out those toxins more gently.

Other chemicals that turn into toxins are taken into the body in other ways, such as through the use of personal hygiene products, such as shampoos, soaps, body products, and makeup. The same applies to chemical cleaners. Many are filled with xenoestrogens, which are man-made compounds that mimic the effects of natural estrogens in the body. They have an effect on health, covering up your receptor sites in the body, and have been linked to cancer and overweight.

You may still have amalgam fillings in your teeth. These are full of mercury and should be replaced. Use toothpaste *without* fluoride, which is becoming to be known to damage teeth and gums.

Sleep

Ensure that you get enough sleep. Go to bed before midnight and get a minimum of six hours (preferably eight) of sleep. No watching TV, gruesome movies, or being on the computer just before bed. Allow at least an hour in between those activities and sleeping. If sleep eludes you, get some advice from a naturopath. Avoid sleeping pills.

If you have difficulty sleeping, take a relaxing bath. Use a few drops of lavender essential oil in your bath, and rub some on the back of your neck as well. Light sleepers may need a totally darkened room in order to get the correct rest. Please: No transformers in radio alarm clocks next to your head. Long-term sleep deprivation can do a lot of harm to the immune system over time, and even create weight gain! Ensure that your bedroom feels relaxing and nurturing to sleep in, and the colors you paint your walls are soothing!

Take Time Out

It is essential that you take time out from your busy schedule and learn how to *relax* so your body can recuperate from the daily stresses. This journey is not going to work for you if you do not learn how to do this and get away from the hustle and bustle of life. Do this regularly during the day. Take five to 10 minutes out every couple of hours, walk away from your desk, breathe some deep breaths, drink water, and even go into nature for a few minutes if you can.

Ensure that you get regular longer breaks from your normal day to day activities. Go somewhere different, perhaps a weekend away with a friend or partner, rest in nature, or go to the sea or mountains for good air for a day or two. A few weeks away for a holiday allows you not only to relax, it allows your body to rejuvenate and recuperate as well!

Grounding with Nature

Get into nature for the pure purpose of grounding yourself with Mother Earth. Take off your shoes and put your feet directly on the earth for a few minutes a day. She has a wonderful balancing energy. If you don't live in the country you will be in environments that are much polluted, and the e-smog will unbalance your electrical field, taking you off your center. Hug a tree and feel yourself absorb its energy and vibration; it is giving you the gift of balancing your electrical impulses.

Remember how good you feel when you have been in nature for the day? Restored and revitalized. If you can get to the sea, treat yourself—or sit by a stream. By the water is where the most relaxation can be had. You are breathing in all those negative ions!

Exercise: Move the Body

Do regular exercise that supports your system. There are times when you push too hard and times when the body needs more restful exercise; be aware of this, especially if you are a gym junkie or runner. A gym in New York does "slow" workouts with its customers. It is said that more results are achieved by doing three half-hour slow sessions per week than the usual three one-hour workouts a week. Interesting?

Maybe do a variety of exercise that gives you both resistance and strength training. Yoga and tai chi are other forms of movement that have more than one benefit; they offer both relaxation and a workout for the body. Walking is an obvious exercise giving your muscles and heart a good workout, especially when you go up hills! Enjoy yourself and play a sport—good for the body, plus the added benefit of connection to others. Have fun with this, ensure that you really enjoy your exercise, and don't make it a chore.

Whatever you do, move and stretch daily. Your body is your temple; treat it with respect and listen to what it is saying. Take in rays from the sun on your long bones if possible; they need the Vitamin D hit.

Body Work

Nurture yourself with regular body work. Choose from massage, acupuncture, shiatsu, kinesiology, cranial sacral, chiropractic, and osteopathy—something of your own choosing. I love the Raindrop Technique, a particular energy massage using essential oils. It works on a very deep level. Other modalities, such as energy healing, work on your energy bodies. (There are many modalities to choose from.) Check into what is best for you and your circumstances.

You need to regularly stretch to unwind your muscles. Move stagnant energy and toxins out of your own body; they come from your emotions, your mind, your physical body, and your spiritual energies. Otherwise the energy gets stuck, and pain builds and persists. The name of the game is to keep those energetic pathways open.

Nurture

Your soul needs nurturing regularly. Ask yourself: *What nurtures me?* Write a list of small things and give yourself a treat often. Is it time to have a relaxing cup of coffee at your favorite cafe, an energy juice full of goodness, a bowl full of your favorite ice cream, some body work, a trip to the park, a walk on a beach, a movie, a cocktail watching the sunset, takeout food for the evening? Once you have started to treat yourself once a week, start listing the items you would like to spoil yourself with on a monthly basis, and then go for the big one on a yearly basis. You will be surprised at what happens once you start receiving.

Hugs, Touch, and Human Connection

Touch and hugs are an important aspect of living day to day. Humans need to be touched as much as they need food and water; touching is energy food for your soul. Many are not in a situation where family or close relationships are available, and living in isolation makes it difficult to get the daily hugs dose. Society is quickly becoming a touch-phobic one, with the introduction of a lot of machine-driven activities.

Touch is needed to feel connection with others. It helps reduce anxiety, helps with bonding with another, lowers your blood pressure, improves your confidence and outlook, and gives the sensory input that our mental and emotional bodies crave. Therapist and author Virginia Satir states that human beings need four hugs a day for survival, eight hugs a day for maintenance, and 12 hugs a day for growth. So start hugging, and hug yourself, too! It reminds me of the story of an Australian guy who went around the world giving away free hugs. Have you seen him on Facebook?

Forgiveness

A big path to loving yourself in the third-dimensional reality is total forgiveness of yourself and others. It is also coming from a place of self-acceptance of what is. Make this a priority as a mind-set you will adopt in your life.

Colin Tipping, in his book *Radical Forgiveness,* asks: *"If there is a divine purpose behind all things which is what is being explored here, is there such a state as forgiveness? Or by working from a higher vibration state of love on the 4ᵗʰ dimensional, which you will come to experience in yourself and others is there such a thing as forgiveness -an interesting proposition?"*

140   Dig Deep & Fly High!

If you come from a space of loving unconditionally, there will be few attachments or situations to forgive as you take responsibility for your life and what you create.

If you get stuck along the way, I encourage you to search out a method such as Ho'oponopono, a Hawaiian Kahuna method of forgiveness or meditation, visualizations, or voice dialogue. (Look on-line for more information.)

This is a favorite of mine, given to me by my yoga teacher. Visualize the person you want to forgive with the intention that you will let him or her be as he or she is, and say the following: *"I release you to the universe. I am free, you are free. I bless you with all my love."* Take a few deep breaths, imagine you are letting the person go, and be still for a little while.

Giving and Contributing

Sometimes receiving from the universe is a difficult process. There can be a block to receiving the energy that is always in abundant supply ready for you. To remedy this situation and unblock the energy flow, I have found if I start to give to others unconditionally, the river opens up.

You can give or contribute in numerous ways. Volunteer in a way that is appropriate for you; help out at a senior's center, or assist at schools or charities and in hospitals. Just give a few dollars to a cause you believe in. I love Kiva, an organization where you support people in third-world countries to start businesses with small micro loans. They are then able to help themselves. Another joy is to help serve Christmas lunch to home-less people. Even a big smile to others you meet along the way is a con-tribution. Pay it forward.

Gratefulness

Be grateful for everything that comes your way. If you let go of your expectations and attachments to an outcome, you will be given an enriching experience in your life. Get into the habit of writing a daily gratitude diary. Write down each evening a few things you are grateful for that were given to you during the day.

It is my experience that you become so busy in your day, you forget to slow down and you miss the small gifts that are given. There are so many things to be grateful for: the colorful flowers that greet your eyes, the air you breathe and the sun that shines, the rain that falls and nurtures the planet, and the birds that fly—let alone what happens to you on a personal basis!

Dreams

Dreams are a way for the subconscious mind to sort out problems, during your sleep period, that you may encounter. Have the intention before you go to sleep that you would like some assistance in sorting out whatever it is. Have a pen and paper at your bedside to write down your insights when you wake. Write them down as soon as you are aware of them whatever the time, as dreams can be quickly forgotten.

Daydreaming

Again, with schedules being busy in today's world, you need space to just be, allow the body to catch up, and give the brain a rest. Daydreaming is a wonderful exercise that allows your creativity to bubble up, and, if you pay attention, will you give you lots of clues of what and where to go next. The shower is a wonderful place for this activity, or swinging in a hammock, or you could get up an hour earlier, have a cup of a healthy beverage, and just be with the early morning with no agenda.

Silence and Meditation

Other ways to support the mind are through total silence and meditation. These help stop the millions of thoughts and eternal mind chatter, and have been found to improve creativity and the thinking process. These are also good ways to practice observing what is going on. They will give you a sense of peace throughout your day. You can practice doing mini (five-minute) meditations to support your stress levels, they will help revive you throughout the day.

Walking in nature or by the sea and dancing are also known to be forms of meditation. Twenty minutes of meditation a day is equivalent to a few hours' sleep. If you are brave enough you could attend a seven- or 10-day vipassana meditation course, where total silence is observed for that length of time. Maybe make it a regular activity on your calendar?

Peace of Mind

For peace of mind, adopt states that support this. Let discernment be your sounding board. KISS: Keep it simple, sweetheart! Make up your own rules. Laugh and see the humor in little things. Drop expectations. Be in beauty daily. Value your vision. Treat you and everyone in a big way and with kindness. Follow your heart. View life with curiosity and innocence. Be the witness and observe from a high plane. Have the courage to accept what is. Trust the universe. Surrender and forgive.

Purification

As you learn to purify your mind, your body, and your energy, you can support this by purifying yourself and home through your different senses, such as through sound, smell, movement, taste, and feeling. It brings a sense of calmness and ritual to the atmosphere.

Another form of deep energy clearing is taking part in a Native American sweat lodge. Dancing is also a form of ritual that is done in many cultures to ward away bad spirits.

Use sound as purification as well. You can use tuning forks, crystal bowls, or metal Tibetan singing bowls, or through meditation with music.

One of the best ways I have found for purification is through the sense of smell. Diffuse essential oils, burn incense, or smell fresh flowers. Also, you can use essential oils on your body.

Indigenous cultures are rich with these kinds of ceremonies, and you may be attracted to this kind of work. Anthony Robbins, author of *Awaken the Giant Within,* uses fire walking as a method of cleansing in his workshops.

Clearing the Clutter

Similar to a body cleanse, clearing your clutter on a physical basis cleanses your space. Remove old photographs that are not meaningful anymore. Clean out your wardrobe; give away clothes you no longer wear. Go into your office, and clean up your files and papers. Give away books or novels to a hospital.

Clean up your children's clutter. Let them help you in the process. Make it a game and give away toys that are no longer needed. Clean out your kitchen drawers and cupboards, and all the other cupboards in your house. Clean the garage, the office, the shed. In particular clean the inside of your car. You will be amazed at how much clearer you will feel in that uncluttered space. Do this at least every six months!

Be aware of one thing regarding old family photographs and ornaments: Do you like them, or are they in your space because a member of your family gave them to you and you do not want to offend? If the latter is the case, you are creating negative energy by having them in your space. Remove and replace them with something more to your liking.

Environment

What is vital and so often forgotten in your life is to keep your space relatively clutter free. Keep the kitchen and dining room tables for eating, not for piling papers. Decorate your home, your bedroom, and even your space at the office with objects that have meaning. Make your space beautiful with items that gladden your heart and bring a smile to your face.

Make sure you are not being affected by transformers in your appliances and that your electrical switchboard to the house is not against any bedroom walls, as it will disturb sleep. Take regular breaks from the computer, keep a proper distance from your TV if it has a plasma screen, and keep mobile telephone usage, especially to the ear, at a minimum. All of these will affect you on an electromagnetic basis, making it hard to keep your energies balanced.

Bring color into your space with your furnishings and artwork. Buy flowers regularly, have plants in the house, light incense, have essential oils burning, and play music you like. Open windows for fresh air to flow. Heighten your senses in every way. Be happy in your space. You have to live there, so make it how you want.

Boundaries

After taking this journey for a little while you will get to find out more about what supports you and what is for your highest good. You may need to start practicing putting some boundaries in place in your relationships and with family members with your communications and feelings. Take responsibility for this one; do not blame others for your own misgivings. They are doing nothing to you. If you are feeling upset about what is going on, look at your reaction and get in touch with the feelings that it has brought up. See where it connects for you. Do some writing on the subject. Get clear about what is really going on for you; only then, when you feel there is no attachment, you are free to go ahead and take the necessary action.

Fear and Stress Support

If you find yourself in a place of anxiety or stress, panic attack, or fear, and you feel you are unable to cope and in need of instant help, take a few deep belly breaths. This will help you calm down initially. This slows your heart rate, and ensures that you are not continually holding your breath, which you often do when panicked or frightened.

Anxiety and Stress: When feeling stressed, sit down, hold one palm across the front of your forehead, the other palm across the back of your head near the base of your neck, and breathe slowly for about two to three minutes. Then drink some water. I think you will feel a little better, and it will take off the edge of the stress.

Panic Attack: If you experience a panic attack, breathe into a *paper* bag for a few breaths. The idea is to increase the carbon dioxide of the air in the lungs, which helps you stop hyperventilating and stabilizes your breathing. If no paper bag is handy, use cupped hands.

Fear: If you get into a fear state or feel trapped, and become paralyzed and over-emotional, you need to expand your energy field around you. You are feeling this way because your normal energetic field that surrounds you has contracted with the fear to such an extent that there is no space around you. Take a few deep breaths, and in your imagination see the energy field around your body expand away from the exterior of you by at least by a meter. Continue to do this until you are calmer and the fear seems not to be so terrifying or overwhelming.

When All Else Fails

Breathe, let go, surrender, and let the flow take you. When you don't know what to do, embrace and feel the void of nothingness, and the feeling that you may have no direction at this time and let the universe support you.

Support

Ensure that you have a support network of people who are glad to help, and who are not into criticism and judgment about what you are doing. Ask a good friend to support you in both the up and down times—someone who will listen with compassion and wipe away your tears, and give you a gentle nudge and tell you the truth when needed! Also, don't be afraid to ask for help when required. It is a human requirement to need loving support.

Examine your motivations around your friendships. Be very honest with yourself. Are these friendships for your highest good? You may need to sack some friends if they are not in that category.

When taking the necessary steps to do the deep inner work and delve into your history to identify the sources of your situation, often a support person (preferably a professional) is necessary to guide you over the bridge of opportunity to the other side where the sun shines!

If you need professional help, guidance, or support, go to a qualified person who has been recommended to you. The key here is to find a person whom you can trust, work with, and be empowered by. Find someone who ensures that you get to the source of your issues, and not just patch up the symptoms.

Network

Spend time and network with like-minded people who have similar interests as you do. Create a strong circle around you. Have fun. If you feel you are short on this one, join a group or a club to help you find people with the same interests. This will support your journey. Everyone needs to belong; it is recognized as a primal need of humans to belong to a tribe, whether that is a family, group, or local community.

Fun

This is another way of nurturing you; it fills you up. Write down what gives you a sense of fun. What makes you laugh? What activities do you love to do? Is it lunch with a close friend when you can let time drift? Having fun with friends? Drinking a cocktail while watching the sunset? Climbing a mountain? Going to a movie? Nurturing you with a massage? Fun is essential in your day.

Just the activity of laughing alone releases lots of endorphins through your body, enhancing your immune system and helping dissipate stress—and it feels good, too! My heart sings when someone smiles at me, and I love to do the same back. If you are a stress bunny, when you start to slow down you will find it comes naturally!

Intentions

Intentions seem to have an element of the intangible to them that we often miss. In our world we are so guided into using our left brain to establish goals that we forget the basic part of this process: to magnetize or draw to us what we want. This is a right brain job! The idea is to become the illumination—the lighthouse, so to speak—so that light attracts or draws to you what you desire. *Desire* here is a word that needs deep feeling, excitement, anticipation, and imagery, and when you add the intangible it often transforms the process into something immediately accessible.

Process: Find a quiet spot in nature or sit at home listening to soft music. Take a few deep breaths and silence the mind. Get grounded. Ask to be given five words that are an *inspiration* to you that are intangible (such as peace, love, joy, etc.). Ensure they are supportive and for your highest good. Chill out *and* have no attachment to what you hear; just listen. Be intrigued by the answers.

Write the five words; then write the first tangible thing that each word represents to you. Now brainstorm the words of what they mean. You have just taken the intangible and put it into a tangible form.

Clarify these into a nutshell and ask: *Who do I have to be to achieve this? And what strengths do I need to pull this to me for it to be so?* You are working backward, trusting your high self to give you the answers so you can follow through.

Self-Inspiration

You need to be inspired regularly; otherwise you become restless and your creativity starts to die. Find activities or hobbies that you love that you can possibly share with others. It may be bike riding, dancing your heart out, taking singing lessons, or singing in a choir. Go out on a trail bike, ride a horse, or take a walk in nature. Relax and read. Improve your knowledge about the world around you; learn a new skill; perhaps take up photography. Attend inspirational events. This activity keeps your mind alert and keeps you interested in life, which will give you overall balance.

Clothing and Appearance

Only wear what makes you feel good. Choose your clothes carefully each day, and let them match your mood. Be playful. Wear colors that enhance your natural hue, and learn what shapes suit you. Don't wear clothes that make you feel old or unattractive, as that is the energy you will put out.

You feel safe in your "old" style clothes. Be adventurous and try something new. (That goes for men, too!) If you don't know about these things, ask a friend to help, go to a store with employees who know what they are talking about, or hire a professional image consultant. When I was working as an image consultant, I was amazed at the transformations that happened through this process.

Writing for Dumping, Questing, and Inquiry

There are three uses for a journal:

1. Write a daily journal of three pages a day. This is called free-form writing; keep the pen flowing. (Preferably do not take the pen off the page.) You are dumping all your thoughts onto paper and out of your mind. Do not get into your thoughts and judgments. If you cannot think of anything to write, write that down. The purpose of this is to empty your mind of all the mind chatter. Do not read what you have written afterward; whatever you have written is just that: writing with no meaning.

2. As a spiritual practice, use writing as an inquiry tool. Ask yourself questions to prompt you in writing non-stop. Choose a word to write about, such as self-love. Write for a minimum of two to three pages.

3. A wonderful method of asking questions if your head is getting in the way is "left-hand/right-hand writing." Use your dominant hand to write a question, and write the answer with your non-dominant hand. I find, with this technique, even if my mind wants to write one thing, what is written as an answer with my non-dominant hand is different. It is like your small child is answering the question; it seems to bypass the ego!

Creativity

Allow yourself to go overboard on developing your creativity. It is your spark. Ensure that you are allowing full expression of this part of you. If you are not sure what your passions are, start something that will ignite the fire. Maybe start art lessons or dance lessons; learn salsa, African dance, or maybe belly dancing. Allow your voice to be expressed and sing in a choir. Whatever you do, have fun with it. These are all things that encourage that part of you to open up.

Vision Board

This is fun to do by yourself or with your partner or your family. A vision board puts your intentions out to the universe. Write out your aspirations and dreams, or listen to your intuition and be on the lookout for signs given. Take time; dream big on a large piece of paper.

Take a large piece of paper or a large piece of canvas board. Choose your context or contexts that this board is about. It could be about your whole life, or it could be about finding a new home! Once you are clear about what it is, write about how this feels to you in a sensory way.

Consider the following: How does it smell? What does it look like? Is it in black or white, or are there any colors involved? How strong are the colors? How does it feel? Is it rough or smooth? Does it have a shape? What is the taste like? Are there any sounds that connect with the vision?

Pick out pictures from magazines or the Internet that give you the feeling of what you have written. Don't be too literal in what you choose. For instance, you may want to have an adventure in a game park. Choose pictures that give you the feeling of what it is you will experience on a more intangible basis that might be adventure. Don't choose a picture of a hippo basking in the sunlight; he is relaxing. Instead choose a picture that gives you the feeling that you are experiencing adventure. Keep it somewhere where you can look at it every once in a while to jog the subconscious about what it is manifesting for you.

I love this exercise. I have often done boards and put them aside, only to look at them a year later and find—bingo—I have experienced most of what is there. This can be done for a broad-spectrum vision of your life or just one area. It gives you great clarity.

***

I have listed lots of different methods and tools to support you on your journey. Choose a few that work for you. There may well be differ-

ent ones that resonate at different times along your journey. You probably have some of your own.

The key is whatever you do, *please support and nurture yourself!!*

Section Four

Bringing it All Together for a Shining Life

Chapter 11

The Next Step:
Designing Your Soul Awareness Guide

Your personal road map

"Our goal while on this earth is to transcend our illusions and discover the innate power of our spirit. We are responsible for what we create, and we must therefore learn to act and think with love and wisdom, and live in service to others and all life."

~ Caroline Myss

*L**et's get started with the steps that you are going to take along the way!* This journey takes your personal commitment, and for you to have gotten this far I know that you have made it! You can get taken away from commitment easily by being distracted by other, more seemingly important things. Just check in once in a while with yourself to ensure you are on track. If you are off, just refocus. It is that easy.

Write a declaration of intention of how you will move forward and take this journey. Writing an intention for this kind of journey gives you a sense of purpose, connects with your inner strength, and aligns your innate intelligence with a direction. When times get tough along the way—and they can—come back to your intention for encouragement. If confused about a decision, ask: Is this supporting my soul's journey or not? You will get a bodily response and the anwer will come to you.

I will share mine with you: "To serve my highest source. I commit myself to a life of loving with an open heart and compassion, fully and completely—I am God, I am Sovereign and I am Free."

Before you start designing your Soul Awareness Guide, make your commitment of intention. Ensure that this will support you on your path.

Now is the time to put your own Awareness Pathway or Guide together that resonates with your very essence and that will develop your spiritual practice. I have included helpful hints to be aware of along the way.

There are *seven essentials* that need to accompany you on your journey, supporting you along the way and that will assist you on increasing your energies: **clearing your clutter, adopting daily habits, daily journaling, tools of the authentic path, silence and meditation, a gratitude diary,** and **a treasure map,** plus reminders of what will support your behaviors, mind-sets, and attitudes.

So far you have been going down the path of exploring the more body-mind aspect of you; now it is time for you to start physically clearing out what is of no further use to you! This is the fun part and is designed to give you a big push.

Start with the seven essentials listed below; they will give you a solid base to accompany you along the way. One of the most important steps— maybe the most important step—is **clearing your clutter** (clearing the physical stuff that you have around). This gives you a head start and will free up your energies and set the scene for your forward momentum.

The Essentials

1. **Clearing Your Clutter:** Start clearing out your physical space, so you can lighten up the energies in which you live and work.

Make a list of everything that you want to clear out in your physical living and working spaces. Don't do it all at once; do it in bite-sized chunks over a few days. That way you keep it manageable and do not go into overload.

This part can be a bit emotional, as there is a story in every piece you are letting go. However, once you are in the swing of it, it can be fun. If you think you need support, ask a friend to assist you along the way. Make it fun!

A hint here: Do not allow yourself to procrastinate or be distracted. Keep your focus. This one step is *important,* as it frees up your energy and gives you the necessary forward momentum as you will see once you have finished.

2. **Adopting Daily Rituals:** Refer to Chapter 10 on supporting yourself along the way. Ensure that you bring together all the pieces of this. Write a list of what to buy and how to do it, and put it by your bedside. If you need to buy some guidance cards, go and choose some. Buy a lovely journal and a pen you enjoy writing with. These are all the necessary pieces to make sure you support yourself in this new way of living. Setting this one in motion starts to build discipline. Your soul will thank and honor you for this.

3. **Daily Journaling:** For some of us journaling is an enjoyable experience. For others it is to be avoided at all costs. (I know, because I was one of those people!)

There are three ways in which to use writing in a journal. It can be used as a purging method, to dig deep and inquire what is inside of you from a deeper perspective, or to support you in finding quick answers to a question.

My advice: If you are in avoidance, journaling is a very powerful way to unearth "stuff" or "baggage" from your deep unconscious, and it also helps and soothes any pain that may arise. Once you have experienced how it works, you will see how it can become your best ally in this quest.

For deeper inquiry into issues that have surfaced during reading this book, regularly go to your Discovery A-Ha's Map, pick items that have that "ouch" factor, and go digging. Work through the things that sit uncomfortably with you.

Similar to the values process, pick the top seven items that you would like to handle and focus on, and get started with your journal. Do this as part of your daily morning pages. You will be amazed at how quickly things come together.

With journaling sometimes the mind goes blank. You can use prompting questions or words that you put up the top of the page, read out aloud, and then just write. Keep repeating the question you are writing about if you go blank again. The key is never to lift the pen off the page until you have written your three pages, regardless of what you write down. And be gentle with yourself; the light bulbs will go off, giving you deep insights.

4. **Tools of the Authentic Path:** Go to Chapter 10. Choose those activities that jump off the page and that will be enjoyable for you. List those that you would like to incorporate into your life, and make a commitment to do so.

   Also choose a couple that you would normally avoid. This is to push you along a little and expand your comfort zone. Get out your calendar, and start to make appointments with yourself to do this.

   Check in regularly and review, as you may like to include others. Do this maybe every one to three months.

5. **Silence and Meditation:** Allow yourself each day periods of silence, preferably at least 15 minutes a day in one sitting. You

could choose to learn different methods of meditation, or even do specific meditations that you find on the Internet. Perhaps take a walk in nature, or even do some Ecstatic Dance. It is this time alone when you come to experience yourself on another level, deep inside.

6. **A Gratitude Diary:** Start a daily gratitude diary. Note each day what has happened in your life that makes you feel grateful. Was it something in nature? Another person's kindness? Even yourself as you start treating yourself with more respect and self-care? As you do this your mind and energy will attract more of the same energy back to you.

7. **A Treasure Map:** This is an ongoing project. A treasure map gives you the impetus of forward momentum; it is like dangling a carrot to your subconscious to start working for you in an uplifting manner. If the universe doesn't know what you would like to create and enjoy, how can it bring it to you? Initially, daydream and write freeform on the nine contexts that we talked about in Chapter 5; I have listed them here again for reference:

   - **Intimate Relationships:** your love life, partnerships, and marriages,

   - **Self-Recognition:** how you see yourself in the world,

   - **Health and Family:** your background history and state of health,

   - **Prosperity, Abundance, and Fortunate Blessings:** how and what you manifest in life,

   - **Creativity and Your Inner Child:** your creativity and childlike playfulness,

   - **Career and your Life Path:** your passions and talents expressed through your work,

- **Inner Knowledge and Intuition:** how well you know you and use your intuition,

- **Support, Helpful Friends, and Fun:** the support and fun you experience,

- **Unity:** your light vibration, balance, energy levels, and general flow.

||||||||||||||||||||||||||||||||||||||||||||||||||||||||||||||||||||||||||||||||||||||||||||

Treasure Map Task:

Get a large piece of flipchart paper; make areas for these on your paper. You may want to do this in a circle form, or freeform, or even in a square of nine areas. Check in with the writing you have just completed and your **Awareness Light Bulbs Map** and **Benefits and Rewards Map.** They will give you lots of clues. Start pasting pictures, symbols, and words that entice you and make you excited.

Put all your wishes and dreams not realized yet. Be clear with yourself that these are current and not old dreams that do not serve you anymore, or somebody else's dream.

Add your **values** to this list, too. Remember that they are your rudder to guide you. Add to it when you want, tick off what you achieve, and put it somewhere you can see it daily, or pull it out once a week and check it over. This is your soul guide for your future, so visit it often!

||||||||||||||||||||||||||||||||||||||||||||||||||||||||||||||||||||||||||||||||||||||||||||

What is useful at this time is write a list of pointers that will remind you of supportive behaviors and attitudes you can adopt along this path. You can also go back to the foundational guidelines of the universe in Chapter 7. I have listed some others below:

- Remember to stay in the present moment, pay attention to what is going on around you, and be the observer—the witness of your life.

- Listen to yourself deeply; messages are being given constantly if you were only silent to your inner voice.

- Become aware of those small thoughts that normally get pushed aside.

- When challenged by others and events around you, take a deep breath and let go.

- Use all your senses and pay attention; feel your thoughts and emotions. Acknowledge what is there and accept it for what it is.

- Be mindful of your actions and how you speak to yourself and others.

- Open your eyes, step back, and see what is around you. Stop and watch the butterfly hover, or the bee settle on a flower, and smell the flower.

- Quit the blame game; you are responsible now.

- Be honest with yourself. You can make a choice in every moment.

- Most of all, be gentle with you. Regain your childlike innocence. Be silent and stop to reflect along the way.

- Have fun, laugh, and be your light in every way.

Another suggestion: find a mentor, guide, or coach to assist and support you. Often when someone else is not emotionally involved, he or she sees your story and your pain, and can hold the space energetically for you to move forward. Sometimes you just need someone to hold your hand for a while as you get stronger. I offer support and programs that assist you in this way. Visit my website (www.YourSpiritualMama.com) for details.

As you go along this journey you will experience new states of being as you start to regain your personal power, your courage, your truth, and your value. The benefits of this will lead you to having more joy, peace, and fulfillment in your life.

Now that you have designed your personal Soul Awareness Guide, you are all set to go on your new adventure. It is that simple. There's just a little bit of organization to do so you do not throw yourself off center and you allow it to guide you. Remember: Nothing is set in stone. It can all change in a blink of an eye!

"...Your soul knows the geography of your destiny. Your soul alone has the map of your future; therefore you can trust this indirect, oblique side of yourself. If you do, it will take you where you need to go, but more important it will teach you a kindness of rhythm in your journey."

~ John O'Donohue, Anam Cara: A Book of Celtic Wisdom

Chapter 12

One Heart, One Spirit

Your soul's calling

"People are like stained-glass windows. They sparkle and shine when the sun is out, but when the darkness sets in; their true beauty is revealed only if there is a light from within."

~ Elisabeth Kübler-Ross

This book has been designed to take you to your cliff edge—to find your mojo. It has been designed to create a bridge for you to cross over into your true life journey, to find out what makes your heart sing, and for you to come to really understand who you are. Your job now is to know yourself, at the deepest level. Remember as a child you were often taught to be fearful of your power. There is nothing to fear.

You have just begun, and for me this journey has been the most rewarding and fulfilling part of my life—to open my heart, start loving myself, and be the love that I am. When you love at this level and you co-create miracles, the magic begins. I offer you a similar experience. I know that this could be your most rewarding journey so far. As a planet I see it as our only way forward.

Please note that when you clear out your old energy patterns and you step through this door to the rest of your life, it is important to have the body-mind in an open state of receiving (like a radio transmitter) to receive your new, upgraded frequencies or vibrations.

As you start the process of letting go of your deep pain, understand you may experience a healing response as your body goes into a detoxification process. Know that this is normal. You are releasing the old energy that has kept you stuck in unhealthy patterns.

As you start to let go of this stuck energy, it becomes freer and your body uses it to heal itself. As a release you may have a cold or flu, or experience being very tired; this is your body releasing the toxins from the physical, emotional, mental, and spiritual bodies ridding the old energetic imprints.

At this time your body needs to recuperate and rest so it can get back to its normal homeostasis or equilibrium. Welcome this with open arms, as it is a sign that you are getting better and that your body is healing. Do whatever feels right (rest, sleep, massage, water, homeopathics and herbs to help it along its way, etc.).

Your energy will slowly return to you, and you can apply this extra zing of energy to enjoying your life. In homeopathy, it is recognized as a healing crisis; you get a little worse before you get better.

The greatest benefit of this journey is learning to open your heart. Your heart is your bridge many more times powerful than your brain. Your higher self is your heart, your essence. It is the connecting place of above and below. When your heart is open, your innate intelligence comes through. It is the momentum in which your body leads you to vibrate to be open to "all that is."

Welcome in the heart love that you are. Come home to your divine blueprint, so you can surrender to loving yourself unconditionally and find internal peace.

"Wake up to your truth. Wake up to your heart. Wake up to your soul. Know your truth. Know your heart. Know your soul."

~ Penelope Aelfin

Chapter 13

The Key: You Are Love

Be it!

"Let there be light.
Let the light be you.
Let there be love.
Let the love be you.
Let there be peace.
Let the peace be you."

~ Guthema Roba

As you awaken to being a fuller human incorporating your divine blueprint, being filled with light and at one with your natural essence, you start to see the world in a very different way. The world starts to reflect back your inner beauty as your life unfolds graciously before you.

When you have more awareness and love for yourself, you have compassion and respect for yourself and others. You come from a place of peace and joy, which naturally exude from your pores.

Sounds good, doesn't it? I believe this is your natural birthright, open to one and all, ready for the taking when you dig deep into yourself, and unravel your history or your story of what you have believed was you. By embracing and accepting both the light and the darkness inside you and dropping your masks, you reach a space when your soul is free, and you fly back home and sit in heart-powered awareness.

You live fully in the moment and give it your full attention. You are the observer in a non-attached way, watching your life flow before you. You surrender to what is, and you are mindful and aware in each moment.

The invitation that is given to you is to start the journey, and it starts with one small step. The journey consists of many such steps and on the way will present you with gifts to explore. Often you are not aware what each step means until you have taken that step. This is a big task, especially if you keep looking at the end point, so keep in mind the final destination is not the goal; it is the joy in the process of the journey of discovery along the way!

This journey will awaken your spark from within, so shine unashamedly! Be the bigness that you are. This journey is where the gifts are given—the diamonds! As you start your journey, bring in your curiosity and sense of adventure, choose to be spontaneous, surrender in each moment, and say *yes* to life! Allow the change, transformation, and transmutation. Your life is a piece of art; live it like a masterpiece and allow your butterfly to emerge from its cocoon.

Open your heart to yourself, and allow yourself to be vulnerable in your feelings. Softness is the key to the opening of the heart and being compassionate. When your heart is open, your vibration ripples out and connects you to the world around you as you learn to live and co-create as one world spirit.

As you release all expectations and self-doubt of yourself, see and be the inner beauty you are. Be your full potential. Express who you are at your deepest level, and express your greatest joy; this is your gift of freedom! Allow yourself to be the well of your own personal oasis, the place of the greatest sustenance.

When you remove the stresses from your life, your nervous system relaxes. Your immune system functions without interference. If any distress does comes along the body corrects itself back to equanimity auto-matically. You were designed to live in optimal health on all levels—physical, mental, emotional, and spiritual—all in total harmony.

This journey takes commitment and courage. When you know in your heart of hearts that your essential nature is made up of particles of light and that you are made up to energy, love, and awareness—all of those things having a human experience—it is somehow easier to play the game of life differently, with a different perspective.

Get to know yourself deeply. Be your own spiritual mama and give birth to your true self. It is your gift and purpose, and you deserve it!

I call it an *adventure of the soul*—almost like a pirate on the high seas of discovery looking for treasures on the way! You will be given gifts along the way that you would not have imagined possible. Be uninhib-ited in your love and love yourself unconditionally. Honor your essence, embody your light, and allow your radiance to shine. In fact, put it first. It is your natural sovereign state—your natural birthright—to be a mem-ber of this human family of love, so claim it and shine!

It would be wonderful to meet you along your journey, and in the meantime I wish you every piece of magic along your way. Enjoy the journey and have fun! Let your light be with you in strength and love, and I wish that many blessings are bestowed upon you on your way.

"Looking behind, I am filled with gratitude,
looking forward, I am filled with vision,
looking upwards I am filled with strength,
looking within, I discover peace."

~ Quero Apache Prayer

How Can I Help You?

"When I stand in the truth of who I am, I no longer fear to begin again."

~ *Tom Lescher*

My experience serves me well to do this work. I hold your hand, nurture you along the path, listen to your story, and assist you to navigate through the maze that maybe in front of you and assist you to integrate the pieces. I serve humanity through understanding love.

I am a teacher, mentor, and guide of universal principles.

To get you started on your journey right away, get your free copy of my *Daily Mindset Reboot* action plan now, "*Stop Being Stuck in The Rut Spinning Your Wheels*". It will keep you out of overwhelm.

It's easy.

Just go to my website at **www.HealYourSeparation.com** and click on the link!

My experience, gained on my own life journey through being physically sick and encumbered, and moving to a new country to experience life differently, made me look into the depths of myself to heal my pain and find my diamond. Working with many clients over the years and seeing them grow into their potential and shine, too, I have something to offer you that will support your soul to come alive and let your spirit shine through.

I support people in finding their real self, giving order to chaos and spotlighting the inner beauty to shine assisting transition through turbulent times.

I offer a variety of packages to support and assist people on their journey. I invite you to check in at my website:

www.HealYourSeparation.com

Some of the benefits you will receive by reading **Dig Deep & Fly High!** *are:*

- Gain clarity about your sacred wounds.

- Receive assistance to look inward to your truth.

- Support you to understand how to take your next steps.

- Help with building a new life for yourself.

- Learn tips and tools of the spiritual journey.

- Follow the path of an experienced traveler.
  Become your own spiritual mama!

I look forward to our journey together.

Go to **www.HealYourSeparation.com**
And get your free copy of my Daily Mindset Reboot
"Stop Being Stuck in The Rut Spinning Your Wheels"

www.ingramcontent.com/pod-product-compliance
Lightning Source LLC
LaVergne TN
LVHW051522080426
835509LV00017B/2161